MANIFEST DAY BY DAY

How to Get the Life You Want, Starting Now

Alanis Cooper lives in London and credits manifesting with having changed her life. Her manifesting videos frequently go viral on TikTok (@alaniscooperx), and she also has a podcast, 'Goal Digging & Manifesting with Alanis'.

MANIFEST DAY BY DAY

How to Get the Life You Want, Starting Now

ALANIS COOPER

First published in 2022 by
HEADLINE HOME
an imprint of HEADLINE PUBLISHING GROUP

1

Cataloguing in Publication Data is available from the British Library

Hardback ISBN 978 1 0354 0101 7
eISBN 978 1 0354 0099 7
Paperback ISBN 978 1 0354 0442 1

Designed and set by EM&EN
Printed and bound in Great Britain by Clays Ltd, Elcograf S.p.A.

Headline's policy is to use papers that are natural, renewable and recyclable
products and made from wood grown in well-managed forests and other
controlled sources. The logging and manufacturing processes are expected
to conform to the environmental regulations of the country of origin.

MIX
Paper from
responsible sources
FSC
www.fsc.org   FSC® C104740

HEADLINE PUBLISHING GROUP
An Hachette UK Company
Carmelite House
50 Victoria Embankment
London EC4Y 0DZ

www.headline.co.uk
www.hachette.co.uk

For my mum, Kathleen – my best friend.

And for my little sister, Jolene:
the world is your oyster, baby girl x

Contents

Introduction

First of all, I just want to say that whatever brought you here today – whether that was a bad break-up, a New Year's resolution or just wanting to become the best version of you – well done you for taking the first step towards changing your life. Manifesting and the law of attraction totally changed *my* life, and it will change yours too! It was March 2020 when I discovered the law of attraction. Boris Johnson had just announced that we were going into lockdown for three weeks and that everyone was to work from home. I had recently experienced my first ever heartbreak, and the way I dealt with this was by constantly keeping myself busy and taking my mind off what I was feeling. So, when lockdown was announced, and we were all told we had to spend three weeks at home (how naïve were we?), I thought that it could be the perfect opportunity to pause and put some time into dealing with what I was going through, with what I was feeling, and start to improve myself. So that is exactly what I did. I then stumbled across *The Secret* on Netflix and have never looked back since.

I have used the law of attraction to manifest some amazing things in my life that I never would have thought possible. For example, I had been constantly researching ways to increase my TikTok following, but had been stuck on 800 followers for around six months. Then I started using a scripting method (I will explain more about this method of manifesting later on in the book), where every day for three days I would write about having 10,000 TikTok followers. Then one day I went out for Sunday lunch and said to my friend, 'I will have 10,000 TikTok followers by the end of today, I just know it!' She had never heard of the law of attraction before, so she was sceptical. Then that night I went home, uploaded a video that got over 2 million views by the end of the night, and I went to bed with 10,000 followers. From then on I knew that manifestation, and actively choosing the dream life that I wanted to live, was really the secret to life. Another example was when I had a £10,000 bill to pay and had absolutely no idea how I was possibly going to get that much money in a short amount of time. Despite this I got to work and started to visualise the money in my bank, I started to listen to money mantras, and constantly acted as though I had the amount in my bank to pay the bill rather than stressing about not having the money. Then one morning I got an email from a brand that I had never worked with or had any communication with before to work for them on a TikTok campaign, and when I got the contract through, the flat-fee rate that they were offering me was exactly £10,000. This wasn't a normal occurrence for me either. I had never been offered a lump sum of money of this amount before, by coincidence the exact amount I was manifesting to pay my bill.

There have been many more amazing things that I have manifested in my life, such as: more TikTok success, exam success, specific opportunities, getting a book deal, bringing out a podcast, a new relationship, new friends and more! So, my manifesting queens, I am going to share with you in this book the exact steps I took, templates for you to follow and any tips I learned along the way while studying the law of attraction.

What is the Law of Attraction?

The law of attraction is the idea that energy flows where energy goes, that our thoughts become things, and that what we put out into the Universe, we receive. Have you ever met someone who's constantly broke, or bad things are always happening to them? This could be because they are always complaining about their situation or living in fear of what the next bad thing to happen to them will be, thus putting their energy into this and attracting more bad things into their life. The Universe doesn't respond to words, it responds to energy; if you are always complaining about your lack of money, then this is what the Universe will provide, a lack of money, keeping you in that same position. 'So how do I manifest more money?' you may be asking yourself. You tell the Universe that you already have it! You believe that you have it and then the Universe will mirror your energy and deliver. The main concept of the law of attraction is actually very simple and the core stages can be described in a simple statement: 'Ask, believe and you shall receive.'

Ask

Think of the first part, 'ask', as ordering something from a menu and being detailed with what you are asking for; for example, if you were to order a steak in a restaurant you would specify to the waiter how you wanted it to be cooked, you would let them know what sides you wanted to order and your choice of sauce. But if you just ordered a steak, it could arrive well done when you wanted it medium rare, and with different sides to what you wanted. Asking the Universe is the same: if you simply ask the Universe to be in love, the Universe may send you a different type of love than the one you are looking for. However, if you ask the Universe for a romantic partner who makes you feel fulfilled and treats you how you deserve to be treated, then this is what the Universe will reflect back into your life. You can do this through the many manifestation methods that I will go on to explain in this book, such as: positive affirmations, scripting, journaling and visualisation.

Believe

This is the second part of manifesting and often the one that people struggle with the most. You have to believe that what you are asking for already exists and that the

Universe is going to bring it into your life when the time is right. If you have never heard of the law of attraction before, it is normal to feel sceptical, as it really does sound like magic. However, it is crucial in order for your manifestations to come to fruition that you believe. A simple way that you can enhance your belief in the law of attraction is by reading *The Secret* by Rhonda Byrne; or if you're not a big reader, you can find the documentary for free on YouTube, and it is also available on Netflix. In *The Secret* there are a lot of people who talk about their experiences with the law of attraction and how they have used it to manifest amazing things into their lives. Seeing all these examples helps enhance your belief and therefore increase your manifesting power. Another thing that I want you to do to increase your belief is to think of either a robin, a duck or a frog. I want you to tell yourself, and convince yourself, that you will see one of these three things, and you could even write in your diary in the past tense, 'I have seen a rubber duck.' Then I want you to let it go and believe that the Universe is already conspiring to bring this to you. Manifesting something small first will help to increase your belief in the law of attraction; you will be surprised how quickly it happens. Once you have manifested this small thing, it will increase your confidence in your manifesting power, which will then allow you to go on and manifest even larger things. The most important part of belief is making sure you do not let your limiting beliefs get in the way. These are the voices in your head that are telling you, 'This will never work' or 'This could never happen to me.' The way that you can eradicate these limiting beliefs is to write them down on a separate piece of paper (not in your journal where you write all your manifestations), then for each one challenge yourself on why you think this. Then when you realise you have no logical explanation as to why this wouldn't be possible for you, burn them safely outside, breathe in and out and let them go.

Action

The action part of the law of attraction is the part that means people can call you smart for achieving all of your goals rather than lucky. The law of attraction is hard work, it requires time, effort and consistency, just like all things in life. You wouldn't go to the gym once and expect to walk out with a six-pack, and it is exactly the same with manifesting and using the law of attraction. In order for your manifestations to come to fruition, it is important that you do a lot of work on yourself, removing any of the blockages that might stand in the way between what you want and how you get there. It requires you to shift your mindset from negative to a more positive one. This book will give you all the steps that you need to help you to do so.

Receive

Now, the receiving part of manifesting is definitely the most exciting part, but the key thing is to truly imagine and visualise yourself receiving your manifestations before the Universe brings them to you. The frequency vibration of receiving will be sent out into the Universe and the Universe will tune into this vibration and this will help your manifestation to transpire. Now, to really do this you need to imagine: who would you tell when your manifestation comes to you? How excited will you be? Will you be jumping up and down? Will you post about it on social media? What will you be wearing? What will you be able to smell? What environment will you be in when it happens? You need to truly transform yourself into the state of abundance and express how grateful you will feel when you receive your manifestations.

Before We Begin

First of all, I want to say again, well done to you for taking the first step towards changing your life by picking up this book. This book is designed so that you choose one area of your life each month and focus on manifesting, with all my tips and tricks, your desires and dreams for that chosen area. If you have an area of your life that you want to focus on first, then feel free to skip to that month and then go back to the previous months. You have the power; you are in control of your own life destiny. On your ongoing manifesting journey, I will be giving you tasks and activities to complete in a journal or notebook, so grab yourself a specific one that you can dedicate to manifesting your dreams and desires. If you have no clue where to start, then following the chapters of this book may be the best thing for you.

The Wheel of Life

There is a tool called 'the wheel of life' that you can use to identify the areas of your life that you are excelling in and putting loads of your time and energy into and also, alternatively, the areas that could do with improvement. I do have videos of this over on my Instagram, @alanis_ Cooper, and on my TikTok, @alaniscooperx, which are examples of my own that I have done in the past! What you need to do is grab a piece of paper and draw a circle. Then I want you to add twelve sections into this circle, like a pie or a pizza, and label each one with the twelve areas of life in this book: love, career, wealth, health, family, education, spiritual growth, friendship, self-love, travel and any other specific goals. Then I want you to rate out of ten how satisfied you are in each area. This is a really good visual tool to highlight the areas that you need to put some work and time into to give you the best possible balanced life, and it can indicate what month you should perhaps start on first. Once you have chosen where you would like to begin, you will work through different activities in this book to come up with some goals for these areas and then, using my tips, manifest them to fruition. It is important that when we are setting these goals that we are setting S.M.A.R.T. goals. This may be something you have heard of in school or used before in your workplace, but S.M.A.R.T. goals stands for goals that are:

Specific: try to be as specific as you can with your goals, especially when using the law of attraction to manifest them; for example, if you want to manifest a new car, describe the colour, the registration year, what it smells like, what the interior is like.

Measurable: your goals need to be measurable so that you can measure your progress to reaching your target; for example, if you just set your goal as 'I want lots of money' without setting an amount, you won't be able to measure how far you have to go and you won't know when you've reached your target.

Achievable: although your goal should be achievable, it should also be something that makes you feel uncomfortable because it is a level up. In other words, set a goal that makes you feel uncomfortably comfortable. For example, if you are trying to manifest money, write down a figure that you feel is easy for you to achieve each month, then write a figure that you feel is out-of-this-world unachievable, and then pick a mid-point.

Relevant: make sure that your goal is relevant to your life and your dreams and desires; for example, if having a ten-bedroom mansion and a Lamborghini doesn't fill you with excitement just yet, then manifest something that does, like having your own one-bedroom flat.

Timebound: make sure when setting your goals that you are setting a time frame in which you would like to achieve them in.

Raising your vibe

The law of attraction states that everything is in constant motion, and everything that is moving has a specific frequency. The Universe responds to the frequency, which is why you need to put out the same high-vibe frequency to the Universe that you would have if you already had your manifestation. You can raise your frequency, or vibe, in many ways.

Express gratitude

The first way is through practicing daily gratitude. Expressing daily gratitude is vital for manifesting our desired goals, as it creates a state of abundance within us and helps to change a negative mindset, where you think you have nothing, into a positive mindset, where you feel full of abundance. This is because we are focusing on the things we are grateful for, therefore focusing on the positives in our life and putting out positive energy. This creates a frequency that the Universe will then mirror into your life. One of the ways that we can practise gratitude is by keeping a gratitude journal. Dedicate an entire diary to all the things that you are grateful for in your life. Keep this by your bed and, when you wake up every morning, before scrolling through your phone, write down at least three things that you are grateful for and why. For example: 'Dear Universe, I am grateful for my comfy bed, as I have a great night sleep in it every night, which gives me energy for the day.' Keeping a gratitude journal also allows us to look back through and realise just how much we have to feel grateful for when we may forget sometimes. Another way that you can practise gratitude is by making a gratitude jar. Grab an empty jar and decorate it however you want – maybe with feathers, jewels or paint. Then, when something good happens in your life that you are grateful for, write it down on a Post-it note and pop this in the jar. This is a fun and simple way to make sure you are celebrating the small things in life, and a good method of picking yourself up when you are having a negative day, as you can look back and remind yourself of all the wonderful things that you have. Another method is listening to songs that make you feel grateful for your life, maybe a song that brings you back to a time where you were in a state of abundance and were truly grateful for life, or a song that says the word 'Thank you' a lot in it, such as the song 'Thank you' by Alanis Morissette. This is a really easy way to practise gratitude without putting too much effort in; you can blare out these songs while driving or doing the chores round the house.

Let go and move on

Another way that you can raise your vibe is through forgiveness and letting go of limiting and negative beliefs.

Holding on to stuff we have not forgiven people for, or past mistakes that we have not yet forgiven ourselves for, is very consuming of our energy and takes up so much of our brain power whether we realise this or not. A way that you can do this is through writing a letter, either addressing it to the Universe or to the people that you hold resentment for and need to forgive, or that you want to forgive you. Detail absolutely everything that you are forgiving them for, their actions, the way it has made you feel, and then end it with the good times you spent with that person as a nice way to remember the positives as well. Once you have done this, although it may be painful, read the letter, allow yourself to feel all those emotions, breathe in and out, burn the letter and let go. You could maybe even put this letter into a text message and send it to this person and let them know that you forgive them or ask for their forgiveness. Although this may be lowering your vibrations for that small period of time, you will have a much higher vibe in the following days and you will feel so free without all these burdens on your shoulder.

Find out what makes you happy and do more of it

Think of the days when you feel really good, when you're on a high vibe. What did you do that day that made you happy? Whatever this may be, whoever you spoke to, do more of it. Sometimes we just need to dance in our rooms where no one is watching, sing from the top our lungs on a car journey or just jump up and down and go crazy to make ourselves feel good. All these things are putting us on that high vibe!

Book time for you

A cliché method of raising your vibe but a very worth-while one is booking time in your diary for a self-care night. We all have such busy schedules and sometimes struggle to switch off and have some downtime. So, block some time out, and allow yourself to be unavail-able. Buy yourself your favourite snacks, put on your favourite series, read a new book, do a hair mask and a face mask and have an early night. You are allowing yourself to relax and rejuvenate, which will raise your vibe for the days ahead.

Meditation

Practising meditation for even five minutes each day can raise your vibration. Meditation isn't for everyone but it can help you to let go of all the chaos going on in your life, be still for a moment and let go of any negative thoughts. You can find specific guided meditations on

YouTube to follow by typing in 'meditation to raise your vibration'.

Reduce screen time

In today's world, it has become so hard to detach from our tiny little screens that seem to be permanently glued to our hands. How many of you are guilty of picking up your phone first thing in the morning and find yourself scrolling aimlessly before your feet have even touched the ground? I know I definitely am! Of course, some time on our screen does bring us joy, such as contacting friends and family and funny videos. However, it is also filled with bad news, and we can end up down a rabbit hole of stalking people who are no longer in our life and looking at people's 'perfect' Instagram posts that can make us think less of our own life. That is why decreasing our screen time can help to raise our vibe, so check your screen time in your settings on your phone and set a goal to decrease it by thirty minutes each day, until you are no longer programmed to pick it up every spare second you get. You can do this by, among other things buying an alarm clock, so you are no longer on your phone first thing in the morning; reading a page of a book each time you go to pick up your phone; putting your phone out of sight and getting a screen-time app on your phone that only allows you to access an app for a certain amount of time each day.

The power of giving

We often underestimate the power of giving, whether that be a gift, a service or just our time. When we give to others it evokes gratitude, makes others happy, enables social connections and makes us feel good about ourselves. And giving is contagious! Through seeing how we can better someone else's life, we have time to reflect and realise how lucky we are to be able to give to someone else. We often feel positive after we have helped someone else, even if it is only a small thing. So, this week think of someone whose day you can make that bit brighter. Perhaps give them a gift to let them know how grateful you are that they are in your life, or send a positive feedback email to a company whose staff has offered you great customer service recently. You could also donate to a charity, feed the homeless or anything else that you can give to help someone else.

Declutter and clean

When we declutter and have an organised home, it is proven to help reduce stress and anxiety, often caused by feeling out of control and overwhelmed. Our homes and especially our bedroom should be our sanctuary, a place where we can relax, a place where we feel in control and safe. Think about the amount of outfits you may have in your wardrobe that you are keeping just in case you ever want to wear them again, or just in case you fit into them again. Organise your wardrobe into categories of what you want to keep, what you want to sell, what you want to donate and what you want to chuck. Then, with the clothes you want to keep, categorise these further into summer, winter, work clothes, daywear and evening wear, and organise everything into your wardrobe this way. This will make your days so much easier by reducing the stress of choosing your clothes when getting ready in the morning.

Now, we all have that drawer in our house that is like an ICT department's cupboard: full of cables and wires for devices that we can't even remember or don't use any more. Go through that drawer and get rid of the wires you haven't used in over a year, because chances are you will never need to use them again! By decluttering and organising our surroundings we are allowing ourselves to be in a more relaxed state of mind, which in turn will allow a higher vibration to flow through us easily and often.

Methods of Manifesting

Now let's talk methods of manifesting.

Method one: manifesting using scripting

So, the first method that I am going to discuss is scripting, and if you haven't heard of scripting before, it is literally taking pen to paper, taking your life story into your own hands, and writing the script of your life. There are many different ways to script your life and these are: journaling, the 3-3-3 method, the 5-5-5 method and the 3-6-9 method. I will explain all these below. The key to mastering the scripting method goes beyond writing things down for the sake of it. When you are scripting your life, think about every single aspect of your manifestation. What you would see, what you would feel like when your manifestation comes into your life, and who you would tell. The hardest part of the scripting method is to remember to let go once you have finished the activity, and this is the part of the process that most people have difficulty doing. Letting go of your manifestation requires you to detach from what you have asked for and having faith in the Universe that it will come to fruition. A good way to do this is to be grateful for the life that you already have and everything that you have in it, and to trust the Universe to work its magic, just like it has brought you everything you have ever desired into your life already. This allows you to go from a state of lack and longing for your manifestation into a state of abundance and gratitude, because we must remember the Universe mirrors the vibrational frequency that you put out into it.

The 3-3-3 and the 5-5-5 scripting method

The 3-3-3 and the 5-5-5 scripting methods are where you choose a specific affirmation relevant to what you want to manifest and then repeat the exercise of writing it 33 times for 3 days, or 55 times for 5 days. An example would be: 'I am so excited that I have received an extra £500 in my bank this month.' You would then write this in one sitting 33 times for 3 days or 55 times for 5 days. Make sure when choosing the affirmation you are going to write that you are as specific as you can be, that you write it in the present tense as if it has already happened and that you try to stay as present as you can when writing it down. Make sure you feel how you would feel when your manifestation comes to fruition, that you align your vibration with how your manifestation coming true makes you feel, and that you let it go. The Universe will pick up on this vibration and mirror it. Neither method is more or less effective than the other, it just depends on how much time you are willing to spend on your scripting method each week.

The 3-6-9 scripting method

The numbers 3, 6 and 9 are believed to be 'divine numbers' by Nikola Tesla and he once said, 'If only you knew the magnificence of the 3, 6 and 9, then you have the key to the Universe.' There are two ways that you can carry out the 3-6-9 method and again there is no way more effective than the other, it is just a personal preference, so I would encourage you to try both ways and see which works best for you and can fit into your lifestyle better. Try to do it every day if possible, or until you truly believe that your manifestation is on its way to you and that the Universe has heard you.

The first technique of the 3-6-9 method

The 3-6-9 method has three separate parts. First of all you need to write the 'thing' that you want to manifest and write this down 3 times, then you need to write the 'action' to do with the thing you want and you need to write this down 6 times, and lastly you need to write down the 'emotion' connected with the thing you want to manifest and write this down 9 times. An example of this could be:

£500

£500

£500

I have £500 received in my bank.

I have £500 received in my bank.

I have £500 received in my bank.

I have £500 received in my bank.

I have £500 received in my bank.

I have £500 received in my bank.

I feel extremely grateful for the extra £500 I have received in my bank.

I feel extremely grateful for the extra £500 I have received in my bank.

I feel extremely grateful for the extra £500 I have received in my bank.

I feel extremely grateful for the extra £500 I have received in my bank.

I feel extremely grateful for the extra £500 I have received in my bank.

I feel extremely grateful for the extra £500 I have received in my bank.

I feel extremely grateful for the extra £500 I have received in my bank.

I feel extremely grateful for the extra £500 I have received in my bank.

I feel extremely grateful for the extra £500 I have received in my bank.

This method is usually preferred over the 3-3-3 or the 5-5-5 method, as it is not as repetitive and it is easier to maintain focus when manifesting your chosen thing.

The second technique of the 3-6-9 method

The second way to use the 3-6-9 method is to write down an affirmation of the thing you want with the action and the emotion – for example, 'I feel extremely grateful for the extra £500 I have received in my bank' – then write this down 3 times in the morning, 6 times at lunchtime and 9 times in the evening. This method allows you to focus on your manifestation three times in that day; however, you still need to master the art of letting go once you have finished the practice.

Journaling

An effective journal practice that you can do to manifest your desires is to put a future date in the corner of a page in your journal – for example, if you wanted your manifestation to come to fruition by the end of the year, you would write 31 December and the year – then continue to write a diary entry as if you are writing on that date. Journal as if everything you want to manifest for that year has already happened. Write down every little detail, who was around you, who you told, how you felt, what you could hear, see, smell; be as descriptive as you possibly can. You could also break down your goals for the year into monthly goals and according to what you have or haven't received yet, write down the end date of the month in the corner of the paper and write down everything you want to achieve that month as if it has already happened. Again, be as descriptive as possible, detailing the emotions you would feel. It is good practice to re-read these diary entries on multiple occasions, with high-frequency music on in the background (you can find high-frequency music on YouTube), and really imagine the emotions you would feel. A good tool is a website called 'Dear future me', and you can find the link to this in the Resources section at the end of this book. The website allows you to write yourself a letter, and you can choose the date that this letter gets sent back to you, whether in one month's time or one year's time. When you re-read this letter at the end of the time frame, you can reflect on all your manifestations.

Method two: manifesting using visualisation

Visualisation is a very powerful and in fact a very easy manifestation tool if you are a big daydreamer like me. You have probably done this a lot in the past subconsciously without even realising that you are manifesting. I know I had before I even knew what the law of attraction was. Have you ever imagined a situation or a scenario happening and then, a few days later, near enough the exact same situation occurs? This is visualisation. Visualisation activates your subconscious, which will then start generating creative ideas for you to act on so you can achieve your goals. It programmes your brain to recognise resources that you need to achieve your dreams and activates the law of attraction. Like scripting, when you visualise you need to be in a high-vibe state – so, for example, after mediation or when you are really relaxed in bed at night. It is important when visualising that you try to be as specific and as detailed as you can, really setting the scene for what you desire your dream life to be. There are a few ways that you can use the visualisation method, which I will talk about now.

The cinema method

This is my favourite visualisation method and is exactly what it sounds like. I want you to imagine you are at the cinema, the lights dim, people go quiet, your phone is on silent tucked away, and then the film starts rolling. The film showing is whatever you want your life to be, whatever you are manifesting. The main character is you. How are you acting? Are you confident, full of abundance, content, living your best life? Or are you still in the position that you are today? Who are the other characters in the film? What qualities do they possess? Are they supportive and proud of you? Or are they jealous and negative? What is the main character wearing? Where are they working? Where are they living? What can they hear? All these small details are the details you need to think about when imagining the person that you want to be when you have received your manifestation from the Universe. This will get it really clear in your mind exactly what it is you want to put out to the Universe and the Universe will get in tune with your vibrational frequency, mirror it and reflect it back into your life. The best time to do this is when your subconscious is most active, which is twenty minutes before you go to sleep at night and in the first twenty minutes when you wake up in the morning. If you are somebody who struggles to visualise exactly what you want, then it may be useful for you to write what you want down in your journal first and try to be as descriptive as possible, thinking about all the small details, so when it comes to visualising you have a better idea of what it is that you are visualising.

Vision boards

The purpose of a vision board is to be a visual aid that will engage your subconscious mind to make your goals and manifestations attainable. There are so many examples of vision boards out there; however, the key to making a perfect vision board is making one that is 'perfect' for you. The images on your vision board must be aligned with your dreams and fill you with excitement. It is also important that when you are adding images to your vision board that you don't just choose ones that are aesthetically pleasing. Make sure they are relevant and as specific to your goals as you can possibly get. Make sure that with every item you are adding to your vision board that you are energetically charging them with your positive energy as you place them and feeling the excitement you would feel if you were to obtain this manifestation. Make sure this vision board is available for you to see every day. There is no point making a vision board and then sticking it under your bed for the next year: it needs to be somewhere where you can feel inspired by it every day. Your bedroom is the perfect place for it so you can see it first thing in the morning and last thing at night.

To make a vision board you'll need a board (you can use a cork board, a bit of cardboard or a foam board), scissors, your images, stuff to attach your images, depending on your type of board, and any materials you want to use to decorate your board. You can also make a digital vision board. Good apps to do this on are Canva, My Vision Board and Pinterest. This allows you to choose your images online and then you can set this as your home screen so that every time you look at your phone you are reminded of your manifestations and your goals. I would recommend doing both these methods so that you are regularly looking at your manifestations and activating your subconscious to think of ideas that can help you attain these goals. You can make a vision board for a specific year or for a longer period of time – for example, everything you want to manifest within the next ten years. The results of vision boards are phenomenal.

Method three: manifesting using positive affirmations

Positive affirmations are positive statements used to challenge and eliminate negative thoughts that can hold us back. The way we use affirmations to work with the law of attraction is through declaring what we wish to attract into our life, and doing this repetitively to reinforce the strength of them. It is very important when using positive affirmations to manifest that we say them in the present tense, as if the Universe has already granted us our manifestation. Later in the book I will go through specific examples of positive affirmations that you can use to manifest great things in each area of your life. But here are some examples of general positive affirmations that you could use to enhance and strengthen your manifesting powers:

- I don't chase. I attract. What is meant for me will find me.

- Thank you, Universe, for always giving me what I want, and for always granting me what I need.

- Thank you, Universe, for matching my vibrational energy and always delivering.

- I am filled with abundance and I am on the path to where I am supposed to be.

- I believe that I am the creator of my own life destiny.

- I am constantly striving to increase my vibration.

- I am increasingly confident in my ability to visualise my desires and make a positive contribution towards them every day.

- I am living a life full of abundance and have many amazing things in my life to feel grateful for every day.

- I am always learning new ways to focus on the positive things in my life, and through doing this

I believe I am on a better path to reaching my life destiny.

- I am giving and receiving all that is good and all that I desire.

- I have the power to create my reality.

- I appreciate all that I have.

- I infuse my day with positivity.

- I am worthy of a great life.

- I aspire to be a blessing and inspiration to others.

- I am motivated to achieve my life goals, overcome challenges and live with passion.

A really beneficial way to use your positive affirmations is to choose one or two to repeat daily for a certain period of time, such as one to two weeks. This way, the affirmation becomes ingrained in your subconscious and your vibrational energy will start to shift. You could do this while you're in bed first thing in the morning, you could do this while you are getting dressed, you could do this while you are driving to work. Another good way that you can make this method more practical, is to record yourself saying the positive affirmation over and over and then you can play this through your headphones when walking in public or working at your desk.

Method four: manifesting using crystals

Using crystals alongside the law of attraction can help us get into vibrational alignment with the crystal, and with our goals. There are many different crystals and many different ways that we can use these crystals to help enhance our manifestations.

Crystals that you can use to manifest love and romance into your life:

- Rose quartz: rose quartz is rich in feminine energy and can help you to get your vibrational energy aligned with the love that we want, in order to attract a romantic partner into your life.

- Amethyst: amethyst is a crystal that can help attract self-love into your life. It is often called the healing stone and can help restore your self-worth and peace in your life.

- Rhodochrosite: rhodochrosite can help you to work through your personal issues that are standing in the way of you meeting life goals. It helps you to sort through your emotions while ensuring that your heart stays open to new love.

Crystals that you can use to manifest wealth and success into your life:

- Citrine: because of citrine's high-vibrational energy, it is really good to use alongside your manifestations for wealth. Keep a citrine crystal in your purse or wallet to get your vibration energy aligned with manifesting money.

- Pyrite: pyrite is known to be 'the stone of abundance' and it helps to remove the feeling of having little money and feelings of not being worthy of money, as it can shift you into a state of abundance.

- Green aventurine: green aventurine is thought to have an opportunistic energy. It can be used to manifest more opportunities into your life that will increase your financial income.

Crystals that you can use to manifest good health into your life:

- Clear quartz: clear quartz possesses the qualities of being able to amplify your energy, aid concentration and help with your memory. It does this through balancing your energetic system.

- Obsidian: the benefits of using the obsidian crystal to manifest better health is that it has been proven to reduce pain caused by arthritis, joint problems and cramps. It obtains the qualities of compassion and strength.

So now we know the different types of crystals for manifesting different areas of your life, I am going to tell you exactly how you can do this. After you have connected with the right crystal, you need to set your intention and think about what you are trying to manifest with this crystal. Write this down on a piece of paper and have this beside you. Then, once you are clear on your intention, you should hold the crystal in your hand and focus on the intention as if it has already happened, using all your senses to imagine what it would be like. Then sit quietly and focus on your breathing, connecting your breath to your intention, to the ground you are sitting on and to the crystal that you are touching. Once you have done this for a few minutes, put the crystal back in its designated place and let go of the manifestation. You should work with your crystal daily, or as often as you can, because the more that you do this, the more vibrationally aligned you are becoming with your manifestation.

Another way that you can enhance your manifestations by using your crystals to work alongside the law of attraction is to think about where you are placing your crystals. For example, if you are looking to manifest wealth or career success, you would keep your crystal at your workplace by your desk, by your study at home, or even in your wallet. The crystals will then work as a magnet for good energy and help us get rid of our scarcity mindset and will help to remove any blockages we have that relate to money.

You can also use your crystals during meditations as this allows you to open up to the frequency of the crystal and to clear your mind. You can do this simply by practising breathing methods while holding the crystal after you have set your intention with the crystal, or you can also do this by following a specific guided meditation for that crystal, which you can find on YouTube. If you feel that holding the crystal will distract you from being in a meditative space, then you can always create a crystal energy field with your crystal. You can do this by placing a crystal in front, behind and on either side of you, allowing yourself to be encompassed by the energies that the crystal is releasing.

As we use our crystals more and more, they may get clogged with any negative energy we omit or that they pick up from our surroundings, so it is important that we clean our crystals at least once a month. You can do this simply by placing them under running water for one minute or you can place them in a bowl of salt water for up to forty-eight hours – this will also recharge the crystal's energy. Other ways to recharge your crystals include holding them under a full moon, burying them in the ground or burning incense over them. Their energies will then be recharged and will be able to maximise your manifestations at full capacity.

Method five: Manifesting using music

Music can raise your vibe and create a shift in your mindset. We often don't realise how powerful the lyrics in the songs we are listening to are, but music has the power to completely transform our energy. You can also use subliminal music. A subliminal is a positive affirmation repeated over and over again, delivered to the subconscious part of your brain. You can find subliminals for manifesting for free on YouTube. Subliminals are great as they require no work and you can listen to these in your headphones at work, while you do the chores or while you are driving. Often a piece of music or relaxing sound such as waves crashing are placed over the loop of affirmations, so that you cannot even hear the messages; however, they will be picked up by your subconscious. This is a good way to programme the subconscious mind.

Month One

MANIFESTING
A ROMANTIC LOVE

Romantic love is something that everyone wants to experience at least once in their life. Some people are really good at finding it, while others may have a 'habit' of finding the wrong partner over and over again. Have you ever met that person who says, 'Oh, I always attract the jerks', 'I always go for the girls that leave me for another guy', or 'Men are trash'. These are the people who struggle to find a long-lasting partner to have a romantic love with. This is, of course, because they are putting out into the Universe that they are not worthy of having a loving partner, and what do we know about the Universe? It always mirrors what we put out. However, this may also be because they have some 'love blockages' in their subconscious mind that they need to get rid of. Our subconscious mind is programmed up to the age of seven; before the age of seven our subconscious mind is active 95 per cent of the time.* So, by that point, we already have a set of beliefs that are set in stone and it becomes very difficult to

* https://medium.com/invisible-illness/the-subconscious-mind-inner-child-explained-511b1ef93c7f

challenge them or to change them. Now, how we get rid of these so-called 'love blockages' is by doing our shadow work. Shadow work is a journaling activity where you work on your unconscious mind to uncover the parts of yourself that you hide away and don't like to acknowledge. I want you to think of your earliest memory of romantic love and how it was portrayed to you. For example, this could be from your parents' or grandparents' relationship, what you saw in films, or what you learned from older siblings. Maybe the relationship between your parents in your childhood was very chaotic, or there was little love between them and therefore you might have the subconscious belief that a romantic relationship should be chaotic or loveless. Perhaps as a child someone left your life who your child self always thought would be around, which may have led you to having attachment wounds. Do you find yourself being anxious in a relationship when your partner's behaviour is a bit off and you instantly think they are going to leave you? Do you try to go above and beyond to please your partner above everyone else, even yourself? Do you gaslight yourself into thinking there is no problem with your relationship when there is? Do you find it uncomfortable to bring up problems with your relationship and talk about how you're feeling to your partner in case they abandon you? Then you may have attachment issues that formed in your childhood, but now your inner child is affecting your adult relationships. You may have been really badly hurt in the past by a partner and now the fear of being hurt again is just too much to even fathom falling in love again. There are many love blockages that we all have, which is okay, but we must work on removing these in order to manifest our romantic love.

Now we are going to set our goals for the romantic-love area of our life. When we set our goals it is important to remember that we can adjust them and expand on them as we go along, so don't see this as a stressful task. Take your time to talk to your family and friends about the sort of thing you are looking for – you may not be in a position where you want a full-on committed relationship, you may just be looking for someone you can have fun with, a no-strings-attached kind of vibe! Whatever it is that you want, try to be as specific as you can when writing these goals, and try to give a rough time frame. It is important to remember that goals don't just have to be set at the beginning of the year for a whole year; you can set goals for a week, a month, a quarter, whatever feels right for you. For example, one of your goals may be that by the end of this quarter you will have taken the plunge and signed up to a dating website and, if you got chatting to somebody that you would like to meet up with, that you will have had the courage to go! The self-reflection journal questions below will be able to help you to figure out where you want to be in your romantic-love area of your life.

A way that we can remove our love blockages is through journaling. I would buy a separate private diary for your journaling, and make sure it's strictly confidential. Here are some journal prompts that you can use to figure out what you really want to manifest in a romantic partner.

Journal prompts for figuring out your ideal partner

1. What are the personality traits of your ideal partner?

2. What would be your ideal date night with your partner?

3. What do you love about yourself when you are in love?

4. What don't you love about yourself when you are in love?

5. The person who hurt you the most was _____ because _____

6. What advice does your future self, who is living your ideal life with your ideal partner, have to give you today?

7. In order to manifest the love of your life, the one thing that you are willing to release from your past is _____

8. In order to manifest the love of your life, the one thing you are open to experiencing is _____

9. In what ways does your ideal partner show you that they love you?

10. In what ways do you show your ideal partner that you love them?

11. What do you think has been holding you back from manifesting love so far?

12. What were the biggest problems you faced in your last relationship?

13. What seems to be a repeated problem in your romantic relationships?

14. Do you believe in soulmates? Or do you have doubts? If so, why?

15. What were the best aspects of your last relationship?

16. How affectionate is your ideal partner?

17. How is your ideal partner's relationship with money?

18. What are your ideal partner's flaws?

19. What is your ideal partner's view on having children?

20. What is your ideal partner's view on getting married?

21. What are your ideal partner's goals in life?

22. How can you release urgency, neediness, or other emotions that block the manifestation of love?

23. Is there anything about love that you want to understand better?

24. What type of relationship did your parents have growing up? Do you want a similar relationship? Why?

25. Write about any past trauma that you suspect is affecting your love life.

When manifesting a romantic love, it is very important that we try to focus on the type of partner that we want rather than a specific person we have in mind, or a specific status or look we want them to have. Try to think about the qualities you want them to possess and how you want them to treat you and how you want them to make you feel.

Manifesting a romantic love using visualisation

We can use our vision board to manifest the type of man or woman we want our partner to be. We can do this by adding qualities that we wish them to possess; for example, 'caring' or 'generous'. We can also add images of what we would like our ideal man or woman to dress like or look like, and if you wanted to get engaged, you could add an image of your ideal proposal or your ideal wedding ring. This way our subconscious is always reminded of the type of romantic love we are after and it will always be on the lookout for suitable candidates and eliminate the people who do not fit our criteria. You could also add images of the type of dates you would like to go on, the holidays, and the gifts that you would like them to buy you. All of this is in your control and by putting them on your vision board you are being very clear and very specific with the Universe about the ideal partner and the romantic love that you are wanting to manifest.

You can also use the cinema technique of really visualising yourself with your partner. If you struggle with this, write it down first, and as always we want to be as specific as we can. Where do you meet this person? What can you hear as they are walking over to you? What is the weather like? What can you smell? What are they wearing? What are you wearing? Do you have a drink in your hand? If so, what are you drinking? What do they sound like? What do they smell like? Have you met them before? Really try to be as descriptive and as visual as you can. Get excited about this moment, allow your energy to match this feeling. As much as it is about meeting our ideal person, it's also about us being our ideal version of ourselves to meet this match. Think about what stage in your life you are at when you meet them. Are you confident in yourself? Have you got your finances sorted? Are you happy on your own? What sort of people have you got around you? Where are you working? You should be thinking about all of this, and about how you are going to get to that stage. What does your romantic relationship feel like? Do you feel all giddy like a teenager? Or is it a more comfortable feeling that you have when you are with this person? You can also visualise the type of dates you go on and what you do for fun in your spare time. Think about who you call to tell that you have met this person. Are your family and friends excited for you? Does he or she get on with your family well? And do you get on with his or hers? By really painting a picture of this relationship you are putting out into the Universe exactly what type of romantic relationship you want. Remember the key with all the manifesting methods, is once you have finished the practice, to let it go. We don't want to give off a desperate energy to the Universe, nor do we want to act like we are lacking love; we want to give off the vibe that we are content in knowing our romantic love is on the way to us and that the Universe will deliver, just like it always does!

Manifesting a romantic love using positive affirmations

If a romantic love is at the top of your list of things that you want to manifest into your life when starting your manifesting journey, then I would recommend choosing a few specific affirmations to focus on saying repeatedly daily for at least a month. Here is a list of general positive affirmations that you can use; however, you can also come up with your own that are more specific to you.

Manifesting a Romantic Love

1. The love that I seek is also seeking me; I now remove any blockages that are in my way.

2. I don't chase, I attract. What is meant for me will find me.

3. I am in a wonderful relationship with someone that treats me right.

4. I am worthy of a healthy, loving relationship.

5. I deserve to be happy in my relationship.

6. My heart is prepared to receive love.

7. The Universe wants the most fulfilling wonderful love for me.

8. Sharing love comes easily to me.

9. I am attracting a real connection into my life.

10. I give and receive unconditional love.

11. I am in a relationship with someone who _____ [*list your ideal partner's qualities*].

12. The Universe is full of love.

13. I am attracting a trusting and loving relationship.

14. I deserve a true partnership with my soulmate.

15. My special someone will come at the right time.

16. I forgive past partners for hurting me.

17. My heart is open.

18. My life is filled with abundance and prosperity.

19. I easily attract loving energy and loving relationships.

20. Love is my vibe.

21. I attract new partners everywhere I go.

22. I have an abundance of people asking me to go on dates.

23. As I focus on the love around me, I attract even more love into my life.

24. It is safe for me to receive love.

25. I welcome love with open arms and reciprocate it.

Manifesting a romantic love using scripting

Using the 3-3-3 or 5-5-5 method

As I explained earlier, we can use the scripting method to literally script our manifestations into our life, and you can do this with a romantic partner, whether you choose to use the 3-3-3 or the 5-5-5 method. You could choose any of the positive affirmations listed above to get yourself on the same vibrational energy that you would obtain when your manifestation comes to fruition and write this down either 33 times for 3 days or 55 times for 5 days depending on which method you decide to use. The key is to make sure that when you are putting pen to paper that you are performing an energetic transfer of what it is you want; make sure you are omitting a high-vibrational energy. And remember, like with all methods, once you have finished the practice, take a deep breath, let go and move on with your day.

Using the 3-6-9 method

We can also use the 3-6-9 scripting method to manifest our romantic love into our life. We can use it to get a specific person to text us (if you must), to manifest feeling a certain way, to manifest a person who has a specific set of qualities, and many other things. A common question that I get asked is, 'How often should I repeat a 3-6-9 practice for the same thing?' And the true answer is that you should do it every day, if possible, or until you truly believe that your manifestation is on its way to you and that the Universe has heard you. I am now going to give you some examples of how you can use the 3-6-9 method to manifest different types of love!

Getting a specific person to text or call you

Step one: First of all, you need to be in a state of calm and try to eradicate all other thoughts that are going through your mind. A great way to do this is by practising the box-breathing exercise: breathe in for four seconds, hold your breath for four seconds and release for four seconds. You should carry on with this breathing technique for two minutes or until you feel in a state of relaxation.

Step two: Next you are going to need to hold your phone in your hand and look at it and really imagine this person's text or phone call coming through. What is their name saved as on your phone, what is your ringtone or your text alert for them? You can even go into your settings on your phone and play your ringtone or listen to your text alert. How does it make you feel? Are you excited? Are you jumping up and down? However it is that you feel, I want you to act it out, even if that means screaming and doing a happy dance like a crazy person alone in your room!

Step three: Now I want you to close your eyes and do the same as step two, and imagine their call or their text coming through. What does the text specifically say? What do they say to you when you answer the phone? And what do you reply?

Step four: This is the part where you put pen to paper and use the 3-6-9 method to manifest your specific person to text or call. I am going to give you an example of how you can do this:

Manifesting a Romantic Love

[Partner's name]

[Partner's name]

[Partner's name]

Has texted/called me saying [input].

Has texted/called me saying [input].

Has texted/called me saying [input].

Has texted/called me saying [input].

Has texted/called me saying [input].

Has texted/called me saying [input].

Has texted/called me saying [input] and I feel ecstatic.

Has texted/called me saying [input] and I feel ecstatic.

Has texted/called me saying [input] and I feel ecstatic.

Has texted/called me saying [input] and I feel ecstatic.

Has texted/called me saying [input] and I feel ecstatic.

Has texted/called me saying [input] and I feel ecstatic.

Has texted/called me saying [input] and I feel ecstatic.

Has texted/called me saying [input] and I feel ecstatic.

Has texted/called me saying [input] and I feel ecstatic.

Has texted/called me saying [input] and I feel ecstatic

Manifesting a romantic love using music

Another method that you can use to manifest romantic love into your life is using music to raise your vibe and create a shift in your mindset. We often don't realise how powerful the lyrics of the songs we are listening to are, but how many times have you been having a bad day and then a feel-good song comes on and completely changes your mood? This is because music has the power to completely transform our energy. Here is a list of recommended songs to listen to when trying to attract a romantic love into your life:

1. Gorgon City – 'Ready For Your Love' (you are literally putting it out to the Universe that you are open and ready for love)

2. Mariah Carey – 'Vision of Love'

3. Ariana Grande – 'Into You'

4. Hayley Reinhart – 'Can't Help Falling in Love'

5. One Direction – 'You & I'

7. Miley Cyrus – 'When I Look at You'

8. Ed Sheeran – 'Shape of You'

9. Usher – 'My Boo'

10. Bruno Mars – 'Just the Way You Are'

Manifesting a romantic love using subliminal music

A subliminal is a positive affirmation repeated over and over again, delivered to the subconscious part of your brain. You can find subliminals for manifesting a romantic love into your life for free on YouTube. Subliminals are great as they require no work and you can listen to them on your headphones at work, while you do the chores or while you are driving. Often a piece of music or relaxing sound such as waves crashing are placed over the loop of affirmations, so that you cannot even hear the messages; however, they will be picked up by your subconscious. This is a good way to program the subconscious mind into being open for love and emitting the frequency to the Universe that you are ready to receive love.

Alternatively, you may already have your ideal partner but your relationship is lacking romance at the moment. So you may not want to manifest a completely new love into your life but improve the relationship that you have. Usually when we start to notice problems in a relationship or faults in our partner, we can't help but fixate on these and all of a sudden we are sending our mind into overdrive and thinking of all the reasons why you shouldn't be together and get into a panic that our relationship is over and that it has gone beyond the point of repair! Of course, sometimes it is time to end a relationship if we are not happy. However, often we can focus on a small problem and it can spiral out of control. When we do this we are putting out to the Universe that we have a bad partner and that the relationship is not fulfilling us and that we are thinking we are going to break up with them. In turn, the Universe is going to mirror and reflect this back into our life and therefore the issues in the relationship will not get better and may ultimately end in a breakup. So even if times are a little tough but you want to stay with them, you need to try to maintain a positive vibrational frequency towards the relationship and your partner. You can again do this through the use of gratitude, journaling, scripting, positive affirmations, the use of crystals and visualisation.

Improving your romantic relationship using gratitude

Over the next month I want you to really focus on this area of your life. Every morning when you wake up, I want you to write down three to five reasons why you are grateful for your partner and the relationship that you two have. This will not only help you to realise how many good elements there are to the relationship, but you are also raising the vibration you have towards your partner and showing that you are in a place of abundance with the relationship and it is full of love and positive vibes.

Improving your romantic relationship using journaling

The questions that I want you to answer in your journal are to promote a shift in your mindset and your frequency that you have towards the relationship, and to reflect on all the positive aspects.

1. What is your favourite thing about your partner?

2. What is your favourite way to spend quality time with your partner?

3. If you could describe your partner in three words, what would they be?

4. What is your favourite memory of you and your partner?

5. If you could be anywhere in the world right now with your partner where would you choose?

6. Where did you and your partner meet? Write about it.

7. What was your first impressions of your partner?

8. What is the most romantic thing your partner has ever planned for you?

9. If you could tell your partner one thing you are scared to tell them, what would it be?

10. Do you and your partner have any inside jokes? If so, what are they?

Improving your romantic relationship using scripting

You can use the 3-6-9 method to improve your relationship with your partner by scripting a life where you and your partner are happy and the relationship is full of love. An example of how you can use the 3-6-9 method is below:

[insert partner's name]

[insert partner's name]

[insert partner's name]

Me and [insert partner's name] are madly, happily in love.

Me and [insert partner's name] are madly, happily in love.

Me and [insert partner's name] are madly, happily in love.

Me and [insert partner's name] are madly, happily in love.

Me and [insert partner's name] are madly, happily in love.

Me and [insert partner's name] are madly, happily in love.

Me and [insert partner's name] are madly, happily in love and I feel content and excited.

Me and [insert partner's name] are madly, happily in love and I feel content and excited.

Me and [insert partner's name] are madly, happily in love and I feel content and excited.

Me and [insert partner's name] are madly, happily in love and I feel content and excited.

Me and [insert partner's name] are madly, happily in love and I feel content and excited.

Me and [insert partner's name] are madly, happily in love and I feel content and excited.

Me and [insert partner's name] are madly, happily in love and I feel content and excited.

Me and [insert partner's name] are madly, happily in love and I feel content and excited.

Me and [insert partner's name] are madly, happily in love and I feel content and excited.

Try to do it every day, if possible, or until you truly believe that your manifestation is on its way to you and that the Universe has heard you.

You can also write a future diary entry by putting a future date in the corner of the page and writing down an account of you and your partner's relationship. Detail absolutely everything that you love about your partner and the relationship that you guys have together. You could detail all the dates you have been on; think about how you felt, what you were wearing, what they were wearing, the surroundings, what you could hear. You could detail how madly in love with you they are and the gifts they have bought for you. Maybe they have proposed to you – detail the ring, the set-up, what they said to you. Write about how happy you make each other, write about all the qualities they are exhibiting, how thoughtful, kind and caring they are being. You can also refer back to this diary entry and get excited, raise your vibrational frequency and reflect this out into the Universe.

Improving your relationship using positive affirmations

Focus on a couple of these and repeat them daily for a week, then select a few others to repeat daily until they are drilled into your subconscious and you are on a higher vibration about your relationship:

1. Me and [*say partner's name*] are so happy in our relationship.

2. I am in a relationship where I am being treated how I deserve to be treated.

3. I am in a relationship that is full of love.

4. I thank the Universe for drawing me to my soulmate, with whom I am living a life full of fun and laughter.

5. I thank the Universe for blessing me with a relationship that makes me the happiest I have ever been.

6. I am so grateful to have a partner that is caring, kind and thoughtful.

7. [*Say partner's name*] is so in love with me and I reciprocate.

8. I love [*say partner's name*] easily and he/she loves me.

9. Love is all around me in everything I do.

10. Me and [*say partner's name*] are soulmates and are planning the rest of our lives together.

Improving your relationship using visualisation

Twenty minutes before you go to bed at night or the first twenty minutes after you wake up, when your sub-conscious mind is the most active, I want you to use the cinema method to really imagine your part in your dream relationship. Think about the steps you two have taken to be there. Are you both laughing and giddy again? What has changed in the relationship to lead you to happiness? Are you now in a relationship with little bickering? What sort of person are you now? Are you less dependent on them? Have you both got your own life going on, but when you are together you are enjoying each other's company? And as always make sure that you are getting excited over this; as you are visualising, make sure you are allowing your body to ooze that pos-itive energy and put it out into the Universe.

You can also add your partner to your vision board, to have a constant visual aid of how you want the relation-ship to be. Add a picture of you two together at a time when you were really happy and then you could even write words surrounding the picture such as 'happy' and 'long-lasting'. If marriage is something that you want in the future, then you could add pictures of an engagement ring near the picture of you two, or the place where you want to get married or proposed to. If you would like to go travelling together, then you can add images of all the different countries you would like to go to. And remember to do an energetic transfer of how grateful and excited you are about these images when you place them on your board.

Improving your relationship using crystals

The crystal that symbolises love, rose quartz, is a healing crystal that emits love vibrations. Once you have charged your rose quartz, set your intention, hold it in your palm and say your positive affirmations for improving your relationship. You could also sleep with rose quartz under your pillow or have it with you when you do your visualisation of what your relationship is going to be.

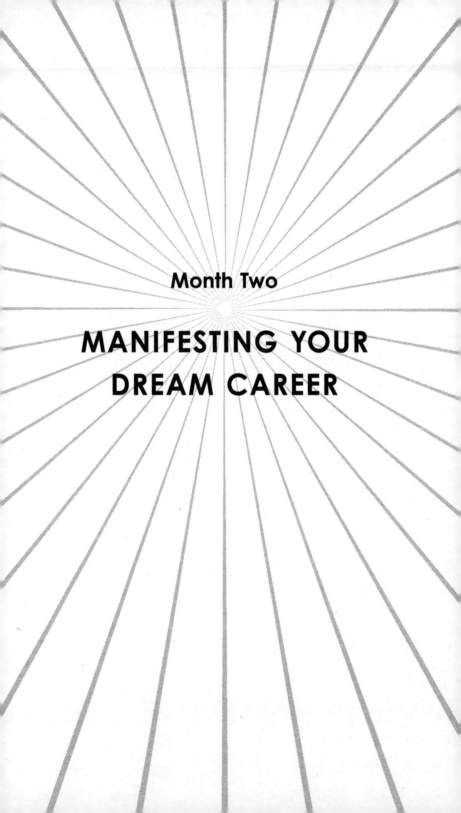

Month Two

MANIFESTING YOUR DREAM CAREER

This month is all about your career, and levelling up in this area of your life. How happy are you with your career or job at this moment in time on a scale of 1–10? If the answer is less than 10, let's put our manifesting caps on and get to work! Did you know the average person spends just under a third of their life working? Your career or whatever it is that you do for work is a huge part of your life, and although not always the case, it should be something that you love doing, not something you dread every time Monday comes around. Of course, not everyone is lucky enough to have job they love, and there are bills and children and other commitments to think about. But what is stopping you from taking control of your own career and finding something that pays well but also works for you? I want you to set some goals for your career, and split these into short term, so for the next year, and long term, so where you see yourself in the next five years. Again, try to make these goals as specific as you can: think about what job title you want, what you want the work to involve, what you want the salary to be and what sort of work/life balance you want. It can be a huge stress setting career goals, but remember these are not concrete, you are not in a rush to make them, and you can change them as your desires and your circumstances change.

I am going to give you some journal questions to answer below. This month in your diary, answer a few each day, be as honest as you can with yourself and remember no one else is going to read these. This is all for you to figure out what it is you want out of your career and to remove any blockages that you may have.

Journal prompts for figuring out your career goals

1. What were your hobbies as a child? If you didn't have any, what sort of activities did you enjoy participating in?

2. List ten ways that each hobby or activity could become a career.

3. As a child, did you like activities that involved working in a team? When you were in the team, did you tend to take the role of the leader? Or did you prefer to be told what to do?

4. What is your desired level of income? Why is it this amount? What would you buy with it and how would it make you feel?

5. The things that I love about my current role
   are _____

6. The things I like least about my current role
   are _____

7. What stresses you out the most about your current
   role that you would like to get rid of in your
   future role?

8. How do you cope under pressure?

9. What is your ideal work environment?

10. I am proud of myself professionally because _____

11. What are your strengths? Are you utilising them to
    the best of your ability in your job?

12. Where do you see yourself in five years?

13. Who is your ideal manager? What qualities do you
    really appreciate in a good manager?

14. List five work environments that you would hate.

15. List the top five companies that you would work for
    if given the opportunity.

16. What is it about those companies that would make
    you want to work for them?

17. Who is your role model? Why have you chosen this
    person?

18. What is standing in between the person you are now and the person you will be once you have your dream role?

19. Who are your ideal co-workers? Describe the qualities that they possess.

20. Do you feel stuck in your current role? If so, why? What is standing in between the role you are in now and your desired role?

21. Write a job vacancy for your ideal job. Describe the skills and qualities needed. The pay. The day-to-day duties.

22. What were your parents' ideal career goals for you when you were younger? Were you socially conditioned into thinking that you had to have a certain career?

23. What is the first thing that you look for when searching for a new job?

24. Have you ever considered having a complete career change? If so, what stopped you from pursuing that change? What are your fears?

25. Describe what you would wear to your dream workplace. How does this outfit make you feel and why?

Manifesting your dream career using visualisation

Visualisation is my favourite tool to use when working with the law of attraction to manifest my personal career goals. This is because there are so many things that you can manifest to do with your career: a salary increase, a promotion, having more responsibilities, winning a big contract, hearing good news after an interview or an exciting new opportunity arising. Receiving the news may be done by an email, or a letter through the post, and what I want you to do is to write a pretend one of these emails or letters and use this as a visual aid to help you manifest the news that you want. You need to make it look as real as you possibly can. If it is a letter you are going to receive through the post, then put it in an envelope and post it to yourself. Lay it out in a standard letter format, so address it to yourself and write your address at the top, have the company logo on there, and sign it from the person that you are expecting the good news from. In the letter include your new job role, the salary, your new title, the start date. Feel yourself getting excited as you type this letter out. Then, when you receive the letter, act as if it is real, feel all the same emotions you will when it comes to fruition, imagine who you would tell. If you want to, you can even take a picture of it and send it to people as if it has already happened. If you are expecting to receive the letter via email, then you can even screenshot this email and set it as your wallpaper so that every time that you look at your phone, you will see it. Read it each time as if it is the first time and feel the excitement, feel that it is real and visualise it into existence.

You can also use the cinema method to manifest progress in your career. Twenty minutes before you go to bed at night or the first twenty minutes after you wake up, when your subconscious mind is the most active, I want you to close your eyes and allow yourself to be transported. Visualise your first day in your new role or new job or with your new salary. Imagine you are waking up on the first day of this new job, what does your alarm sound like? What time do you get up? Is it light outside? What do you do smell and hear when you first wake up? What is the weather like outside? What does it feel like when your feet touch the floor and you know that today is the start of your new future? Visualise every single step that you take that morning to get ready: brushing your teeth, having a shower, making breakfast. Think about the butterflies you have in your stomach, visualise the journey to work, how do you get there? Is there traffic? Are the trains busy? Are you receiving an abundance of good-luck messages? What happens when you arrive at the workplace? What are you wearing? What does the building smell like? What can you hear? Who greets you? Imagine the activities that you will be doing on that first day and how excited and proud of yourself you are.

Then, as always, let these thoughts go and trust that the Universe will bring this to you in divine time.

There are many ways that we can use our vision board to manifest our desired career. Remember that a vision board is a visual aid that constantly reminds us of our goals and triggers our subconscious to find ways for us to get there. The vibration energy that we give off when looking at our vision board will also allow the Universe to tune into our frequency and deliver our desires to us. One way you can decorate your vision board is by printing off the logos of companies that you would like to work for or work with; you could even print off a qualification that you would like to gain in order to get your dream career; print off a picture of the ideal city you would like to work in; print off pictures of the clothes that you would like to wear to your ideal job; make a pretend wage slip with the amount of monthly income that you would like to achieve and print this off. If you would like your own business, print off pictures of what you would like to have your own business in. These goals will then be prominent in your life. Choose images that make you feel inspired to keep working towards your career goals and make waking up for work every morning worth it because you know you are taking the small steps to get your desires. Make sure your vision board is placed somewhere in your eyeline where you will see it daily and, every time you do, spend a few minutes closing your eyes and feeling how excited you will be when your manifestations come to fruition.

Manifesting your dream career using positive affirmations

When practicing the law of attraction, it is vital that positive affirmations are incorporated into your daily routine. If manifesting your dream career is something that you want to focus on this month, then you will need to choose some positive affirmations to repeat daily for the duration of this month, to create a mindset shift and a positive vibrational frequency around your career. A great way to do this is to record yourself saying your chosen affirmations and then listen to this recording on repeat. Here is a list of positive affirmations that you can use to manifest your dream career:

1. I am in control of my career's journey.

2. I am worthy of the success in my career that I desire.

3. I don't chase. I attract. What is meant for me will find me.

4. I am a magnet for amazing career opportunities.

5. Thank you, Universe, for always listening to me and presenting me with the skills and opportunities I need to level up my career.

6. I am grateful to wake up every day and work in a career that I love.

7. I am forever expanding my skill sets and levelling up in my career.

8. Every interview I do takes me closer to my dream job.

9. I deserve to be happy in my career.

10. I am full of abundance in my career.

11. My high-vibrational energy attracts the right career opportunities to me with ease.

12. I am capable of achieving my career goals.

13. I am focused and passionate about excelling in all areas of my life.

14. I am the master of my own career destiny, and I use my time wisely.

15. I have got the job at [*input your dream company*], and I am thriving.

16. I am earning [*insert dream salary*] a year, and this comes easy to me.

17. I am a valuable asset to my company.

18. I am excelling in my new role as [*insert dream job position*].

19. I can be anything that I want to be, and the possibilities are endless.

20. I am always attracting so many new job opportunities that I have to turn them down.

21. My inbox is full of exciting opportunities for me to excel in my career.

22. My career possibilities are endless.

23. I am surrounded by people who support my goals and push me to do my best.

24. I am confident in my job.

25. The path I am on is leading me to where I am supposed to be.

Manifesting your dream career using scripting

Using the 3-3-3 or 5-5-5 method:

As I have explained earlier, you can use the scripting method to literally script your manifestations into your life, and you can do this with your dream career, whether you choose to use the 3-3-3 or the 5-5-5 method. Choose any of the positive affirmations listed above to get yourself on the same vibrational energy – for example, 'I am grateful to wake up every day and work in a career that

I love' – and write this down either 33 times or 55 times, depending on which method you decide to use. The key is to make sure that when you are putting pen to paper that you are performing an energetic transfer of what it is you want; make sure you are omitting a high-vibrational energy. And remember that, as with all methods, once you have finished the practice, take a deep breath, let go and move on with your day.

Using the 3-6-9 method

We can also use the 3-6-9 method to manifest our dream career. Once you have set your goals, you need to think about what's the main 'thing', part one of the 3-6-9 method, that you want to manifest. So, that would be whatever you decided needs to change in your career so you can live your desired life after answering the journal prompts on the previous page. You need to write this down 3 times. Part two is the action relating to your manifestation, so perhaps you have received a call from the interviewer to let you know you got the job, or you received an invitation to a meeting to discuss a promotion, or you received an email with the opportunity that you are trying to manifest, or you got a new contract with a salary increase. Decide what this is then write this down 6 times. The third part is the emotion or feeling associated with this manifestation coming to fruition; do you feel elated, content, proud of yourself, grateful?

Write this down and repeat this step 9 times. An example of how you can do this is below:

New job at [insert dream company name]

New job at [insert dream company name]

New job at [insert dream company name]

I have received a call from HR at [insert dream company name] and they have informed me that I have got my new job.

I have received a call from HR at [insert dream company name] and they have informed me that I have got my new job.

I have received a call from HR at [insert dream company name] and they have informed me that I have got my new job.

I have received a call from HR at [insert dream company name] and they have informed me that I have got my new job.

I have received a call from HR at [insert dream company name] and they have informed me that I have got my new job.

I have received a call from HR at [insert dream company name] and they have informed me that I have got my new job.

I have received a call from HR at [insert dream company name] and they have informed me that I have got my new job and I am so full of abundance and proud of myself.

I have received a call from HR at [insert dream company name] and they have informed me that I have got my new job and I am so full of abundance and proud of myself.

I have received a call from HR at [insert dream company name] and they have informed me that I have got my new job and I am so full of abundance and proud of myself.

I have received a call from HR at [insert dream company name] and they have informed me that I have got my new job and I am so full of abundance and proud of myself.

I have received a call from HR at [insert dream company name] and they have informed me that I have got my new job and I am so full of abundance and proud of myself.

I have received a call from HR at [insert dream company name] and they have informed me that I have got my new job and I am so full of abundance and proud of myself.

I have received a call from HR at [insert dream company name] and they have informed me that I have got my new job and I am so full of abundance and proud of myself.

I have received a call from HR at [insert dream company name] and they have informed me that I have got my new job and I am so full of abundance and proud of myself.

I have received a call from HR at [insert dream company name] and they have informed me that I have got my new job and I am so full of abundance and proud of myself.

Repeat this every day or a couple of times a week – there really is no strict rule, just whenever feels good for you. As always with all the manifestation methods, once we have felt all the emotions connected with our manifestation and raised our energy, it is time to take a deep breath, let go and know that the Universe is working on bringing our manifestations to us.

Manifesting your dream career using crystals

If you are looking to be promoted to a managerial role in your career, then the crystal lapis lazuli can help you with manifesting wisdom and authority. You could place your lapis lazuli on your desk at work, which will allow you to take in the energy that it gives off and put it to use there. It can also be there as a symbol to remind you of what your goal is. You can also meditate with your lapis lazuli: first you must set your intention with the lapis lazuli, then place it in your hand, and bring yourself to a state of calm; you can do this by using the box-breathing exercise: breathe in for four seconds, hold your breath for four seconds and release for four seconds. You should carry on with this breathing technique for two minutes or until you feel in a state of relaxation.

Once you are in a state of calm, allow yourself to connect with the crystal, connect with your intention and connect with the ground you are sitting on, which will allow the Universe to tune into your vibrational frequency. Let the crystal be a mediator for you to connect to your higher consciousness.

The tiger eye crystal can bring good luck into one's life and helps you to make better decisions about your future and the next steps in your career. Again you could place this crystal in your workspace and use its presence to guide you when making business decisions. If you ever feel stuck with decisions about your career, you could meditate with your tiger eye by listening to a guided meditation on YouTube for this particular crystal. Hold the crystal in your hand while listening and this should help you to have a clearer mind and make better decisions that are suited to you. Remember it is important to make sure that we cleanse and recharge our crystals at least once a month as they pick up negative energy from us and can get blockages, which we must get rid of in order to restore them to their natural state.

Manifesting your dream career using subliminal music

The type of subliminals that you may want to listen to when trying to manifest your dream career are ones that relate to your confidence and being a magnet for new opportunities. To see an effect from using subliminals it is important that you listen to the same one on repeat for at least two weeks; this will allow the subconscious part of your brain to be reprogrammed into being alert for new opportunities around you and will affect how you see yourself as a worthy candidate for that new leap in your career. You are also, without realising, radiating this energy to the Universe and, like the Universe is very good at doing, it will mirror and reflect your manifestations into your life.

Month Three

MANIFESTING YOUR DREAM FAMILY

This month's chapter is all about family. For a lot of people, family is the where we call home, where we feel safe, the people we turn to in times of need, and the people who we spend some of the best moments of our life with. The American politician Brad Henry said that our family is our compass that guides us. 'They are the inspiration to reach great heights, and our comfort when we occasionally falter.' Family doesn't always have to be our blood relatives; it can be the people we choose to call our family. Our family is a huge presence in our life, and often we forget to appreciate the time we have with them until those moments become a memory. We have no choice over what family we are born in to, but we do have some control over the relationship that we have with them and the time we set aside in our busy schedules to see them. As we grow older and our list of commitments grows, family can get pushed aside, but it is important that we try to commit time to see the people who always have our back. You may think because you live with your parents that you see them a lot, but I am talking about quality time, letting them know that you appreciate them and that you are grateful for their presence in your life. I understand that some people may not have a great relationship with their blood relatives or may have had a traumatic upbringing. In this case it is important for us to address these issues, to discover and clear any blockages we have around our ideal family, in order to help us manifest a good family unit for when we go on to have our own family one day. I want you to do some journaling exercises over this next month to work out what goals you want to set to improve your relationship with your family.

Journal prompts for figuring out your family goals

1. What is a core childhood memory that you remember about your family? Describe this, go into detail.

2. When is the last time you planned a whole day out with your parents/grandparents?

3. What is your family's favourite way to spend quality time together?

4. List ten reasons why you are grateful for your mum.

5. List ten reasons why you are grateful for your dad.

6. What is your relationship like with your siblings? Have you grown closer over the years? Why?

7. Which of your family members do you get along with best? Write down the reasons why.

8. Are you closer to your friends or your family? Why?

9. What is the most important thing you have learnt from your parents?

10. How well do you know your grandparents? What similarities do you have with them?

11. What is one lesson that you have taken away from your parents' parenting that you do not want to repeat with your children?

12. Talk about the meaning of 'family' to you. Is it more about the people you are blood related to or chosen loved ones? How has your parents' perspective impacted your views?

13. What was your family home like growing up?

14. What is the most trouble you ever got into with your parents when you were growing up?

15. Were your parents strict growing up? Do you wish they were more/less strict?

16. What qualities of your mum's do you see in yourself? For each quality list whether it is a good or a bad thing.

17. What qualities of your dad's do you see in yourself?

For each quality list whether it is a good or a bad thing?

18. Does your family have any traditions? If so, describe your favourite one. Why is it your favourite?

19. What were birthdays like in your house growing up? What is your favourite memory as a child from all your birthdays?

20. Tell me about the family member who inspired you or supported you in a huge way. Have you ever said thank you? Write them a letter to let them know. And if you want to, you can read it or post it to them.

21. Our family values are _____

22. The best gift I ever gave a family member was _____

23. Going forward, would you like to spend more time with your family? If so, how can you make time for this in your busy schedule?

24. Imagine you are describing your family to someone who has never met your family before. What would you say?

25. You can only keep one memory about your family. Which one would you choose and why?

Manifesting your dream relationship with your family using visualisation

Now we have set our goals for improving our relationship with our family, I am going to tell you the different methods that you can use to manifest your family desires with the law of attraction. If there has been a recent fallout with a family member and you are desperate to make amends and resolve your issues with them, you can use the good old cinema technique to manifest the peace and harmony in your relationship once again. So what you need to do is for twenty minutes before you go to sleep or for twenty minutes after you wake up in the morning, when your subconscious part of your brain is the most active, imagine you and that person having the conversation where you speak about why it is that you are not talking any more. Imagine where this conversation is taking place. Is it at a place where you two used to spend time together a lot? Visualise that you are getting to say your side of what happened, and how you feel about things; you get to apologise, and you express how much you have missed them. Imagine that the other person listens to you, sees where you are coming from, apologises too and says that they have missed you as well. Then I want you to go on to visualise all the things that you two enjoy doing in your spare time with each other. Imagine telling the rest of the family that you two have made peace and imagine you are all happy, thriving and spending quality time together again. Ensure that you are sending out to the Universe positive vibrations around this relationship, showing gratitude for this person, and then trust that the Universe will tune into your frequency and deliver to you your desire, as it always does.

You can also use your vision board to imagine this person in your life again. Put up pictures of them on your vision board and keep your vibrations high and positive when you are doing this, instead of looking at the pictures and feeling down. Sprinkle your positivity over them and truly know that the Universe will bring them back to you with divine timing. As always make sure that your vision board is placed somewhere where you will see it regularly, so that it is prominent in the subconscious part of your brain that you have a good energy about your relationship and that this will be restored.

Manifesting your dream relationship with your family using scripting

If you are wanting to make amends with someone in your family and want your relationship with them to be closer again but are too afraid to reach out, then you can use the 3-6-9 method to manifest them reaching out to you; this could be through a text message or a phone call. It is crucial when using the 3-6-9 method that you don't just do this method once; you need to keep at it and put the effort in, just as you would at the gym – you don't walk into the gym, do one workout and then walk out with your dream body. It takes practice, determination, and faith. It is also important that you keep your vibrations high, even if this manifestation takes a while to come to fruition; make sure that you keep your belief in the Universe's work and that your manifestation is on its way to you. I am going to give you an example of the practice that you can carry out below:

[Person's name who you want to reach out to]

[Person's name who you want to reach out to]

[Person's name who you want to reach out to]

[Person's name who you want to reach out to]
has texted/called me to say sorry.

[Person's name who you want to reach out to]
has texted/called me to say sorry.

[Person's name who you want to reach out to]
has texted/called me to say sorry.

[Person's name who you want to reach out to]
has texted/called me to say sorry.

[Person's name who you want to reach out to]
has texted/called me to say sorry.

[Person's name who you want to reach out to]
has texted/called me to say sorry.

[Person's name who you want to reach out to]
has texted/called me to say sorry and I feel grateful.

[Person's name who you want to reach out to]
has texted/called me to say sorry and I feel grateful.

[Person's name who you want to reach out to]
has texted/called me to say sorry and I feel grateful.

[Person's name who you want to reach out to]
has texted/called me to say sorry and I feel grateful.

[Person's name who you want to reach out to]
has texted/called me to say sorry and I feel grateful.

[Person's name who you want to reach out to]
has texted/called me to say sorry and I feel grateful.

[Person's name who you want to reach out to]
has texted/called me to say sorry and I feel grateful.

[Person's name who you want to reach out to]
has texted/called me to say sorry and I feel grateful.

[Person's name who you want to reach out to]
has texted/called me to say sorry and I feel grateful.

Another scripting tool that you can use to manifest making up with this family member, is to print off a picture of them, or simply look at a picture of them on your phone, and below the picture write down absolutely everything that you are grateful for about this person.

Think about all the things that this person has done for you in the past, all the times that they have brought you happiness, what you love about them and why you miss them. Sprinkle that magic (gratitude) all over their name. Radiate positive energy out to the Universe about them and keep your vibration high.

This month you may want to manifest some different family goals, such as starting a family, or being a more present parent in your child's life. The law of attraction can help us with these things and, as always, it will take consistency and time. Everyone's situation is different, and I am not saying that the law of attraction can override the advice the doctor gives you, but if manifesting a pregnancy is something that you want to focus on this month, then it has worked miracles for people before and you should definitely try the below practices. However, please make sure that you are still following your doctor's guidance. There are many different methods that you can use and I would recommend that you use a mixture of them all daily.

Manifesting a pregnancy using journaling

First of all, we are going to focus on our limiting beliefs and blockages. I want you to write down a list of every negative belief you have had around pregnancy in the past, such as: 'I wouldn't have time for a baby' or 'I am not strong enough to be a mother'. Then go down the list, and I want you say to each item the 'Ho'oponopono' Hawaiian prayer, which is: 'I'm sorry. Please forgive me, thank you, I love you.' Take a deep breath and let it go. Writing this list can bring out a lot of raw emotions the first time you do it, but the more you declutter your negative thoughts around this subject, the more the Universe will work with you to bring you your manifestations. Each time one of these negative thoughts pops into your head, take a deep breath, forgive yourself, go through the list and say the 'Ho'oponopono' Hawaiian prayer to each item again.

Manifesting your own family using visualisation

First, find a place where you can be alone, and remember visualisation works best when your subconscious mind is most active, in the twenty minutes before you go to bed or the twenty minutes after you wake up. Imagine yourself holding your new healthy baby. Use your senses: what can you hear? is the baby cooing? are you talking to them in a baby voice and telling them how proud you are to be their parent? What can you smell, that newborn baby smell? Can you smell baby lotion? What can you see? What gender is the baby? Do they have your eyes? Are they wearing a fresh white baby grow? Can you see a parade of congratulation cards on the side? Is there a partner standing next to you with their arms around you both? Is your family there? Or is it just you and your precious bundle of joy? Imagine how content and happy you are feeling in this moment, like it was all worth it. You need to make sure that you really believe that this will be your life one day, and, as always, my manifesting queens, take a deep breath in and out, know that the Universe is getting to work and that this will be your life one day.

You could also use your vision board to send subliminal messages to the Universe that it is in your destiny to have your own family one day. You could add pictures of your ideal family from Google or a picture of you and your ideal partner with some children around it. You could write words on your board such as 'healthy, happy baby' or 'family', or you could add pictures of a scan to manifest a pregnancy. As always, make sure your vision board is placed in sight so that you can see it regularly and feel full of gratitude each time that you pass it.

Another thing that you can do is buy a baby grow. If you are trying to manifest a specific gender, then buy a baby grow for the gender that you are trying to manifest, and hold this while you visualise.

Manifesting your own family using positive affirmations

Choose a couple of the manifestations below to focus on this month and repeat them daily. You can change them up each week, but it is important to be consistent, so it may be useful to set a time each day when you will do this – for example, while making breakfast or while commuting to work. You could even record yourself saying them and then play them on a loop. This will allow you to have a mindset shift, from a negative mindset around having your own family to a positive one, and it will raise your vibration.

1. I am taking care of my body and my mind in order to welcome a baby.

2. My body is designed to conceive.

3. My body is a fertile space.

4. I am grateful for my body and all that it does for me.

5. I am worthy of a baby.

6. I still have time to conceive.

7. I will be the best parent ever.

8. I have a healthy, happy baby on the way to my arms.

9. I trust the process.

10. My body is capable and strong.

11. I am safe.

12. My thoughts are peaceful and calm.

13. I am calm and not in a rush.

14. My time will come.

15. I will be a loving parent.

16. I will do all that I can to take care of my baby.

17. Pregnancy is possible for me.

18. I love holding my baby in my arms.

19. I love my little family.

20. I am loving my life as a mother.

21. Being a parent is the best gift of all.

22. Everyone is so excited about my good news.

23. I have a healthy pregnancy.

24. I am grateful for my and my baby's health.

25. I now have everything that I have ever wanted.

Manifesting your own family using scripting

This month, if you are focusing on manifesting your own family, then you may want to purchase a candle that is associated with the smell of a newborn baby – for example, clean laundry. The glowing radiance of the lit flame will radiate a powerful and positive energy into your home. Once you have lit your candle, do some breathing exercises and ensure that you focus on your breath and try to clear your mind of all negative thoughts. Then set your intention of wanting to manifest having your own family, get out your manifesting journal and perform the 3-6-9 method.

First of all you need to write down what you want to manifest 3 times, then you need to write the action to do with the thing you want and you need to write this down 6 times, and lastly you need to write down the emotion connected with the thing you want to manifest and write this down 9 times.

New baby

New baby

New baby

I have just given birth to a healthy and happy baby.

I have just given birth to a healthy and happy baby.

I have just given birth to a healthy and happy baby.

I have just given birth to a healthy and happy baby.

I have just given birth to a healthy and happy baby.

I have just given birth to a healthy and happy baby.

I have just given birth to a healthy and happy baby and I feel so grateful and content.

*I have just given birth to a healthy and happy baby
and I feel so grateful and content.*

*I have just given birth to a healthy and happy baby
and I feel so grateful and content.*

*I have just given birth to a healthy and happy baby
and I feel so grateful and content.*

*I have just given birth to a healthy and happy baby
and I feel so grateful and content.*

*I have just given birth to a healthy and happy baby
and I feel so grateful and content.*

*I have just given birth to a healthy and happy baby
and I feel so grateful and content.*

*I have just given birth to a healthy and happy baby
and I feel so grateful and content.*

*I have just given birth to a healthy and happy baby
and I feel so grateful and content.*

It is important with scripting that you try to do this every day that you can remember. It doesn't matter if you forget one day, just be sure to keep doing other easier methods, such as affirmations and your gratitude, to keep your vibrations high around the topic of getting pregnant. And ensure that each time you perform the method you aren't just writing your manifestation down for the sake of it, that you are really putting yourself in the future and feeling all the positivity and excitement that you would feel when you do give birth to a healthy and happy baby. As always, at the end of practising any manifesting methods, our last step is to let go, and give thanks to the Universe for always listening to us and for everything that we already have and for always delivering to us what we want.

Another scripting method that you can use is writing a diary entry for five years' from now. So, in the corner of your page, put today's date but with the year five years in the future. Document how you found your pregnancy, or how you found adoption, how you find being a parent, how old your baby is now, what your favourite thing about being a parent is and the challenges you have overcome but wouldn't change for the world. Be very descriptive; try to document as much detail as you can. Who's around you, is there another parent helping you out? Where are you living? Are you in the same house that you are in now? Or have you up-sized? Write about your characteristics as a parent. Are you strict? What values do you try to instil in your children? What is your favourite thing to do as a family in your spare time? Do you spend a lot of time in nature? Do you spend a lot of time at work? Do you spend a lot of time at home? Really try to imagine yourself having that parent role and how you would act. Once you have completed your diary entry, you can always pin it on your vision board, and read over it throughout the month, making sure each time you do you are feeling the excitement in you emerge and that you're emitting positive vibes.

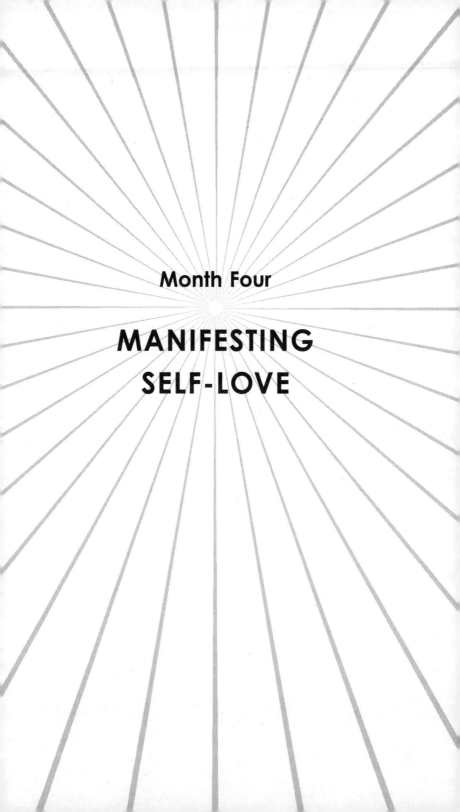

Month Four

MANIFESTING
SELF-LOVE

This month's intention is something that we can all agree we need little bit more of – and that is self-love. From a young age we are often surrounded by people saying, 'Oh, she loves herself' in a negative way, which is ironic, as many of us struggle with self-love. Social media is filled with influencers telling us to love ourselves, but self-love is a lot more than the cliché pamper night or looking in the mirror and telling yourself you are worth it, even if you don't believe it! Self-love is so much deeper; it's a journey and it doesn't happen overnight. Self-love is putting yourself and your needs first, being unapologetic about who you are, being non-judgemental about yourself and being kind. Having self-love and knowing your own self-worth will do incredible things for you in all areas of your life. It will give you the confidence and belief that you can do anything you put your mind to, it will stop you allowing people to treat you less than you are worth, and it will make life so much easier when you're not constantly worrying about others' opinions.

Before we set our goals, as always, we are going to delve deeper into our subconscious and really assess everything we feel around our self-worth. You may have more self-love than you realise or you may actually be lacking it.

Journal prompts for figuring out your self-love goals

1. What is your biggest achievement to date? How does this make you feel about yourself?

2. What makes you unique compared to everyone else?

3. Name three flaws about you that you accept.

4. What is your biggest struggle with loving yourself? And what can you do about it?

5. Write yourself a thank you letter.

6. Write down a hundred reasons why someone would be lucky to date you.

7. Why are you proud of yourself?

8. I need to let go of _____

9. What is the best compliment you've received?

10. How do you feel when you get compliments from strangers? Do you struggle to accept them? Why?

11. What habits do you have that keep you comparing yourself to others? How can you let these habits go?

12. What negative beliefs do you have about yourself? List them below, and question each one.

13. What are you ashamed of? Then write below that you are sorry and that you forgive yourself.

14. What habits do you have that make you feel bad about yourself? How can you replace these habits with ones that make you feel good about yourself?

15. When do you feel best? Can you fit this into your schedule more?

16. What labels do you give to yourself?

17. What do you need to start saying 'yes' to?

18. Write out a perfect night-time routine? What is stopping you from practising this every night?

19. What boundaries do you need to set for yourself?

20. What is your favourite thing about your body?

21. My best personality trait is _____

22. If your friends were to describe you in three words, what three words would they use?

23. Write a letter of advice to your younger self.

24. Write a letter of advice to your future self.

25. Would you be happy if someone spoke to you the way you speak to yourself?

These journal prompts may be tough to do at times, but this will all benefit your self-love journey and help you to realise where you can be kinder to yourself.

Manifesting self-love using visualisation

Think of somebody you know; they could be a celebrity or just someone you know at work who has amazing self-love and oozes confidence. Now, this isn't an activity for you to compare their physical appearance or their achievements with yours, but to be inspired by their ability to not give any f***s what anybody thinks about them! Think about the way they walk into a room, the way people perceive them, how they take no shit from anyone, the way they dress and the way that they carry themselves. You can put this person on your vision board and write down their qualities that you would like to adopt, so that each time you look at them you are inspired by the type of person you would like to be. Keeping your vision board in a place where you will see it regularly will help these goals be prominent in your subconscious mind, a constant reminder of the type of relationship you are looking to manifest with yourself.

Another visualisation technique that you can use to manifest self-love is the cinema method. You should do the cinema method for twenty minutes before you go to bed or for twenty minutes when you wake up, when the subconscious part of your brain is most active. Close your eyes and imagine the film starts rolling and visualise yourself as your dream version of you. The version of you that loves themselves unapologetically, who realises their self-worth and just how special they are, who is full of confidence and doesn't let any limiting beliefs get in their way. Think about what you're wearing. Maybe you're dressed in a way that you have always wanted to dress but have been too worried about what other people may think; maybe you've got the new job position that you have always been too scared to go for because of your lack of confidence; maybe you are with your dream partner who treats you like royalty and loves you right because you love yourself right; maybe you look in the mirror and feel so much more confident in your own skin because you have stopped comparing yourself to airbrushed pictures on Instagram. Whatever your goal is this month for self-love, imagine yourself in this position, feel the positive energy around you and let the positive vibrations flow!

Manifesting self-love using positive affirmations

The reason we often have low self-worth is because of the negative beliefs we have about ourselves. The use of positive affirmations can help shift this negative mindset into a positive one. This month, focus on saying these positive affirmations daily while looking at yourself in the mirror and watch as you fall back in love with yourself again, or for thew first time. Again, you can record yourself saying these on your phone and listen to these while you are on the go.

1. I love every single inch of my body.

2. I am unaffected by the judgement of others.

3. I am on my way to becoming the best version of myself.

4. Anyone would be lucky to date me.

5. The words of others do not affect me.

6. I am in control of myself, I am in control of my life.

7. I forgive myself for all the unkind things I have said about myself.

8. I promise to be kind to myself.

9. I make the decisions in my life.

10. It is healthy for me to set energetic boundaries and only do the things that I want to do.

11. I am beautiful inside and out.

12. I am proud of myself for all I have achieved and all I am yet to achieve.

13. I have big dreams for my future and I am excited about the journey I will take to get there.

14. Nobody is me and that is my power.

15. I am different, and that's what makes me me.

16. If anybody is negative around me, I reflect their energy back, and don't take it personally.

17. I am strong, I am beautiful, I am kind.

18. Everybody I know is lucky to have me in their life.

19. I am capable of anything I put my mind to.

20. I have the fire and passion in me.

21. I was made to receive great things and live a great life full of fun, laughter and opportunities.

22. I am a magnet to all things great.

23. The world is my oyster.

24. I deserve kindness.

25. It is in my power to choose to love myself.

Manifesting self-love using scripting

This month I want you to write a letter to your younger self. Imagine you age five; how you would speak to this earlier version of you? I bet it would be much kinder than the way you speak to your adult self, but why? You are still this little child in this adult body, and this child is counting on you to be kind to them. First of all, tell five-year-old you everything you love about them, tell them how much you love them, and list all of the amazing things that they are going to go on and do in their life that will make you proud. Now tell them about all the hardships that they are going to go through, and how they will deal with them, how they will feel about them once time has passed and the lessons that they will learn. You will start to realise how truly amazing you are and how well you have handled yourself in the past, and instead of feeling sad that you had to go through these things, you should start to shift your mindset to feel gratitude for all the lessons that you learnt. Now write the child version of you a promise that you'll try your best to embrace all their beautiful qualities, to be kind to them, to take care of their body, to push them to their potential and grab every opportunity with open arms!

Using the 3-3-3 or 5-5-5 method

Choose one of the positive affirmations around self-love above and as well as saying this every day, you can write this down 33 times for 3 days or 55 times for 5 days; it really doesn't matter which method you use, just whatever one you find works for you best. Remember each time you write your affirmation to feel the excitement and to radiate this positive energy into the Universe and to act as if you already feel confident and powerful.

Using the 3-6-9 method

First of all you need to write down what you want to manifest 3 times, then you need to write the action to do with the thing you want and you need to write this down 6 times, and lastly you need to write down the emotion connected with the thing you want to manifest and write this down 9 times.

Self-love

Self-love

Self-love

I am full of self-love and know my worth.

I am full of self-love and know my worth.

I am full of self-love and know my worth.

I am full of self-love and know my worth.

I am full of self-love and know my worth.

I am full of self-love and know my worth.

I am full of self-love and know my worth and this makes me feel confident and powerful.

I am full of self-love and know my worth and this makes me feel confident and powerful.

I am full of self-love and know my worth and this makes me feel confident and powerful.

*I am full of self-love and know my worth and this
makes me feel confident and powerful.*

*I am full of self-love and know my worth and this
makes me feel confident and powerful.*

*I am full of self-love and know my worth and this
makes me feel confident and powerful.*

*I am full of self-love and know my worth and this
makes me feel confident and powerful.*

*I am full of self-love and know my worth and this
makes me feel confident and powerful.*

*I am full of self-love and know my worth and this
makes me feel confident and powerful.*

Try to do this every day that you can remember. It doesn't matter if you forget one day, just be sure to utilise other methods, such as affirmations and your gratitude, to keep your vibrations high. And as always when we are doing any form of manifestation, make sure you truly believe what you are writing, get excited as if it has already come to fruition, put out positive energy around self-love to the Universe, and when you are done, breathe in and out, let go and thank the Universe for always giving you want you want.

Actions that you can take to manifest self-love

Although it is the cliché way that everyone talks about self-love these days, pampering yourself from time to time can be nice. Now, that doesn't have to be expensive spa days and buying yourself designer bags, but at least one evening each week this month, schedule into your diary a night where you will do what you want to do, and you will put yourself first. This could mean coming home from work and popping your pyjamas on straight away and closing the blinds and binge-watching Netflix, or treating yourself to an expensive takeaway for one. Whatever it is, make sure you are putting you first!

Another thing that you can do is unfollow anybody on social media who makes you feel like SHIT! As good as social media is at bringing people closer together, it can also be a very toxic place full of airbrushed highlights of people's lives, which, if you compare your life to these glimpses, can be very damaging for your self-confidence. Or you may follow an ex-partner's relation who is constantly posting pictures of them and their new partner, which makes you feel rubbish about your own life. Get rid of all these people, and if it is too awkward to unfollow them, then mute them. You are in control of the stuff you see on your timeline day in and day out, so make sure it is stuff that makes you feel good about yourself!

Manifesting self-love using crystals

The beautiful pink crystal rose quartz is known for being associated with love. It is the emotional crystal for unconditional love – and what better person to manifest unconditional love for than yourself. You can use the rose quartz crystal with a candle to manifest self-love. First of all, after you have cleansed and charged your crystal, light a candle and do some breathing exercises, such as the box-breathing exercise: breathe in for four seconds, hold your breath for four seconds and release for four seconds. You should carry on with this breathing technique for two minutes, or until you feel in a state of relaxation. Place the crystal in your palm and focus on the beauty of the glow from the candle and your crystal. Set your intention of finding unconditional love within yourself. Then feel the positive vibrations the crystal is giving off, and take in all of the love.

Month Five

MANIFESTING
WEALTH

This month we are going to focus on a topic that is seen as 'taboo' by many – money! You'll be happy to know that, in my opinion money, is the easiest thing to manifest, and it was one of the first areas I worked on when I started manifesting. The results were OMG out of this world! I tripled my income within the first two weeks, and before this my only income was from my employer. I was completely and utterly blown away by how powerful the law of attraction was. Financial freedom is a common goal shared by all, yet only very few people that we know achieve it. These are often the friends or family members about who we say, 'Ah, they just got lucky' or 'They were in the right place at the right time!' but never 'How can I get to their position?' or 'I am going to put my mind to it and live a life just as lavish as theirs'. Although we say 'money doesn't buy happiness', if I was given the choice of one million pounds or to have the best relationship in the world with my mum, I'd choose the one million pounds. (I am joking, Mum! Although I doubt you are reading this because you'll have just bought the book to support me and post on Facebook, and not got this far into it!) However, money can be a great tool to buy us freedom, the freedom to work when we want and spend as much time with our family as we can, freedom to buy our loved ones whatever their hearts desire for Christmas, freedom to pack up our bags and treat the family to the Maldives! The reason that not everyone feels that financial freedom is in reach and only for the lucky few is to do with the misconceptions we are brought up with around money. How many times as a child did your parents say, 'Money doesn't grow on trees!' or 'The only way you will become rich is to win the Lottery' – not true! Maybe you grew up in a family where your parents were tight with money and were always pestering you to turn off the lights and to not flush every time you went to the loo if it was only a wee. Or maybe you grew up with parents who had a spending problem and you constantly heard your mother say 'Put it on my credit card', or 'I'll buy that out of the catalogue', or those dreaded debt letters were always coming through your front door. All these preconceived ideas around money are installed into the subconscious part of our brain, which isn't our or our parents' fault, as it's likely what they heard from *their* parents, but it doesn't need to be passed down to your children. You can be the one to break that chain! Money is just an energetic transfer between two individuals, and you need to set your energetic set point of how much it is that you want to receive a month or a year. For more information about energetic setpoints, I recommend Denise Duffield-Thomas's book *Get Rich, Lucky Bitch!*. Now, all this might sound scary and completely mind-boggling to you at the moment, because you simply can't fathom how you can earn more than your monthly salary, or you were always taught that 'Only those who work really hard become rich.' Working hard is one way to wealth, but so is working smart, knowing your value and being open to receiving an abundance of money! But don't worry, my manifesting queens – if you follow my guidance in this book, you too will be able to get that bread!

There are so many ways that the Universe is sending us money, without us even accepting it and being grateful for it. There may be a bag of clothes that still haven't been returned that is just sitting in the boot of your car waiting for you to take it to the post office, or there may be spare change around your house that is just sitting in a bowl waiting for you to use. How many of you have been cleaning out your bags before and actually thrown out copper change? I know I am guilty of this! There may be money sitting in your PayPal account that you haven't withdrawn or acknowledged because you don't see it as real money. For a while I was letting my income from my TikTok views just build up and never expressed gratitude or withdrew it and just neglected it! You may have gift vouchers just sitting in your purse from Christmas that you keep forgetting to use, you may be due a tax rebate but just can't be bothered to cash the cheque in! There may be monetary value vouchers on your Tesco club card that you haven't even realised are there because you have never downloaded the app. I want you, this month, to find at least one neglected income of yours and make sure you appreciate it and express gratitude for it, and to note down every single free thing or income that you receive. Because by not doing this we are literally putting out to the Universe that we don't appreciate the money we have, which will not bring more wealth into our life!

Now, of course, like every other area of our life we manifest our dreams and desires in, we are going to revisit little seven-year-old us to remove those limiting beliefs and money blocks. A plea for all parents out there: please save your child the wrist ache of doing twenty-five journal entries a month in their adulthood to remove their blocks that stand between them and their desired life!

Journal prompts for figuring out your wealth goals

1. What is your earliest memory of money?

2. How was your parents' financial position when you were younger? How did this affect you?

3. What is the one thing you want to change for your kids compared to the money situation your parents had when you were young?'

4. How much money do you have left over each month? And how much money would you like to have left over? How can you raise this amount? What is stopping you from having this? Do you spend too much? Are your expenses too high? If so, write a list of your weekly/monthly expenses and try to look for things you can cut down or substitute for a lower price.

5. How much are you earning a month now, and what amount do you need to earn a month to live comfortably? Think of ways that you can try to increase this amount.

6. What hobbies do you enjoy doing? Write a list. Then go through the list and see if there is any way that you can monetise these things.

7. Pick three words that describe your attitude towards money.

8. What's the best piece of money advice that you have ever received?

9. Is there something you could do to make you more money that you are avoiding because of your fear of failure? This could be investing, starting your

own business, or asking for a promotion at work.
Or changing careers?

10. How would having your ideal level of income change
your life? What things would you do differently?
And what things would you do the same?

11. Do you have any money stresses? And if so, how do
you deal with these? Do you avoid them? Do you face
them head-on? Do you think you could handle these
in a better way? Tell me more.

12. What advice would you give to your younger self
about money management?

13. Describe what financial freedom is to you.

14. What was the first big thing that you bought with
your own hard-earned money? How did this make
you feel?

15. What was the first gift you bought someone with
your own money? How did this make you feel?

16. What kind of relationship do you have with money?
Are you a spender or a saver?

17. What do you feel guilty about in regard to your
money?

18. Do you stop yourself from attending social events
because of lack of money? How does this make you

feel? How do you tell people you can't come? Do you say you are too broke? Or do you let them know that you would prefer to do a more budget friendly activity instead?

19. Do you have a budget? If yes, do you stick to it? If no, why haven't you? Is this something you have been avoiding? Do you think that this will help you?

20. What is your ideal way to generate income?

21. Do you believe you are able to be as rich as you desire? If no, then why?

22. What are some things that you tell yourself about money? Are these things always true?

23. Does your current debt outstanding scare you? How much is it? Are you ready to face it head-on and make a plan to minimise it?

24. Where would you like to be financially in five years' time?

25. Describe what being 'rich' means to you?

These journal prompts may be very difficult and raw for some of you to answer, but in order to manifest wealth this month it is vital that we look into these blockages that we all have, and the limiting beliefs that these generate that are standing between you and your dream amount of wealth!

Manifesting wealth using visualisation

Visualisation with money is exciting, as you can get very creative, and there are endless possibilities of where you can go with your money journey. Instantly when it comes to visualising money, people start going down the route of all the material things that they want, such as a new pair of designer shoes or the newest sports car on the road. However, we are going to go much deeper than this because, as you should know already, around here we don't do things the quick way! Remember always that money is an energetic transfer between two people, and that is what we are going to focus on in this visualisation task. This month I want you to document every single penny you receive, because if we are not being grateful for all the small random bits of money we are getting, or all the stuff we are receiving for free, we are simply not putting out into the Universe how grateful we are for it and that we want to manifest more into our life. Then, with every single penny that you receive, I want you to take a minute to close your eyes say 'thank you, thank you, thank you' to the Universe for this and visualise what you are going to spend it on. You can even do this with anything free that you receive; for example, if you receive a free coffee, you can visualise what you would spend the £4.50 (if it's from Starbucks, say) on. Feel how excited this energy exchange makes you and ooze gratitude out into the Universe. Your vision board is also another visual aid that you can use. Think about what your desired level of income is that you are aiming for this month or even year, then print off a blank cheque that you can get from Rhonda Byrne's website (I have put the link to this in the Resources section on page 247), which is signed by the Universe. On this cheque, write down the amount that you wish to receive, the date that you wish to receive it and your name. You can print off a couple of these if you wish, and post one on your vision board, place one in your purse, place one on your desk at work (if you can take the weird looks from your colleagues) or wherever you will see it every day. In fact, this month I want you to try to remember every day that when you see your cheque, you say: 'Thank you, Universe, for my abundance of money.' It's these little habits and routines that you build that will soon shift your mindset into a positively wealthy one. You can also print off your money goal, which is what you are going to spend your money on: maybe you are saving up for a deposit on a house, or to travel the world, pay for your wedding, have a little bit of extra cash each month to put towards fun days out or to have better-quality food. Whatever your specific goal is, print it out and slap it on your wall, queen! Another way that you can use visualisation is actually mentioned in *The Magic* by Rhonda Byrne, and this is to get a paper note and write 'thank you, thank you, thank you' on the front of it, and keep this note in your purse at all times. Every time you see this, read the words out loud, and by doing this you are projecting gratitude for wealth into the Universe. Lastly, you can use my favourite method, the cinema method, as you guys should know by now if you've been reading these chapters consecutively. Use this method for twenty minutes before you go to bed or for twenty minutes after you open our eyes in the morning. Imagine you are in the cinema, the camera starts rolling and you can see your life once you have manifested your wealth dreams and desires on the screen. Let's think about where are you when you get the news that you have received your new energetic set point income. There are lots of things to think about when setting the scene: where are you when you receive the news? How is the news delivered to you? Is this via an email about an exciting new opportunity, or on your website, where you can see an increase in sales of your product or service? Is this in a meeting with your manager, where they tell you that you have been given a pay rise? The next thing you need to think about is how do you feel when you receive this news? How do you act? Do you jump up and down with excitement? Who do you call first to let them know? What is their reaction? As always, be as creative and as specific as you can. Now you need to imagine your life with the desired wealth that you manifested and what it means to you. Do you have more free time? If so, how are you spending it? Are you going to the gym more? Do you have more time to watch your children's school plays and join their school PTA? Do you have more time to do that hobby that you never had time to do before? What do you spend your money on? Are you more generous with your money? Are you donating more to charity? Do you have a cleaner now? Do you have an assistant? Do you finally live in that dream house of yours? Really visualise you living this life. How do you feel? Are you less stressed? Are you so grateful? Do you feel super proud of yourself? And remember, as always once we have used our visualisation tool, that we need to let go, trust that the Universe is bringing our money to us and feel grateful!

Manifesting wealth using positive affirmations

Do you know someone who is constantly moaning about being broke, or about how much debt they are in? And they never seem to escape this trap, and more parking fines and bills keep coming to them? Well, now you know more about the law of attraction, it should seem obvious that this keeps happening to them because this is what they are putting out to the Universe. It is so important that we act optimistic about money and have a positive relationship with money. This month's positive affirmations are, of course, all about manifesting that dollar! By now you should know how your positive affirmations work best for you and fit into your routine, unless you're prioritising this chapter first. If you have a busy routine and are always on the go, you may like to record yourself saying your positive affirmations and then play this on a loop when you are driving, or sitting at your desk, or you may want to fit them into your morning routine and say them when you are brushing your teeth or making breakfast. You do you, queen! Whatever works best for you, keep it up and this month focus on your money manifestations.

1. I am a money magnet, and money comes to me easily.

2. It is safe for me to have a large amount of money.

3. I am worthy of a large amount of money.

4. I release all resistance around attracting money.

5. I am open to receiving unexpected money

6. I am capable of managing large sums of money.

7. I am responsible with my money and manage it wisely.

8. I will be debt free; I have the power and the energy to make it happen.

9. I am in control of the finances in my life.

10. My desires around money are currently on their way to me.

11. The Universe is working to bring me an abundance of money.

12. Being rich is in my nature.

13. It's easy for me to change my money story.

14. I am so grateful for receiving [*say amount*] this month!

15. I am so proud to have sold [*say amount*] of my products this month!

16. I am constantly hitting my money target and my goals!

17. There are so many opportunities for me to make more money in my life.

18. The money that I have invested in myself will return to me tenfold.

19. Money comes to me in so many surprising ways!

20. I choose to only think positive thoughts about money.

21. Money is a great and powerful tool.

22. I bless all rich, wealthy and abundant people.

23. The more I give, the wealthier I become.

24. Money is energy, therefore money is good.

25. I radiate prosperity, money and wealth.

Manifesting wealth using scripting

For each and every one of you, your money manifestations will be different, the amount you are trying to manifest will vary and the method of how you receive this money will vary too. So you can use the 3-6-9 method and make it relevant to you. First, the 'thing': this could be a promotion, the amount of sales you need in order to hit your target, or a bonus at work. Second, you need to do the action, so this is you getting the news that you have received your manifestation. The third thing is the emotion connected to how you feel once your manifestation has come to fruition. Here's an example for you guys if you are trying to manifest an increase in your income each month:

[insert amount]

[insert amount]

[insert amount]

This month I have received [insert amount].

This month I have received [insert amount].

This month I have received [insert amount].

This month I have received [insert amount].

This month I have received [insert amount].

This month I have received [insert amount].

*This month I have received [insert amount]
and I am grateful.*

*This month I have received [insert amount]
and I am grateful.*

*This month I have received [insert amount]
and I am grateful.*

*This month I have received [insert amount]
and I am grateful.*

*This month I have received [insert amount]
and I am grateful.*

*This month I have received [insert amount]
and I am grateful.*

*This month I have received [insert amount]
and I am grateful.*

*This month I have received [insert amount]
and I am grateful.*

*This month I have received [insert amount]
and I am grateful.*

It is important with scripting that you try to do this every day, if possible. It doesn't matter if you forget one day, just be sure to utilise other easier methods, such as affirmations and your gratitude, to keep your vibrations high.

Manifesting wealth using crystals

For my manifesting queens who love a crystal, you will be happy to know that there are an absolute load of crystals that you can use to help bring wealth into your life. You could place one in your wallet, you could place one on your work desk, on your bedside table or you could choose to sprinkle your whole house with them and really maximise the positive energy around money that they radiate. You can also meditate with your crystal. First make sure that it is cleansed and charged, then set your money manifestation intention, hold the crystal and really focus on the crystal you are holding and your money manifestation.

The types of crystals that you can use to manifest wealth:

- **Citrine** – helps to unblock all our limiting beliefs, unlocks our potential and allows us to approach life with a can-do attitude.

- **Green Jade** – has been throughout Chinese history to attract wealth. Green jade has a soft vibration that allows you to keep calm and not make rash decisions.

- **Amethyst** – keeps you connected to your spiritual side and will be good for you if you are a person who has a lot of money concerns, as it will keep you calm and connected to your dreams and desires.

Manifesting wealth using music

There is an amazing money mantra song that is so addictive that I promise you it will be stuck in your head for days without you even having to consciously try to sing it. It is called 'Ching Ching Money Tree' by Ni$h Nasty, and you can also find it on YouTube if you are not 'down with the kids' and on TikTok.

I promise after two minutes you will know all the words by heart and won't be able to resist singing it around the house. You can also hold coins in your hand and shake them to the beat while you are listening to it or singing it! The first time that I listened to it I was completely hooked and had it on all day while I was driving round running my errands, and that night I got my first ever paid collaboration proposal for TikTok. Since then, when I am focusing on manifesting money, it is my go-to listen and I seem to find random money flying at me!

But there are so many songs that you can blast out in your home or when you're driving or on public transport to help you manifest your riches and fortune! Below is a playlist of songs that you can compile for this month and you can even name your playlist with a positive affirmation of your choice, such as: 'I am a money magnet!'

Playlist for manifesting that dollar:

- Abba – 'Money, Money, Money'

- Pet Shop Boys – 'Opportunities'

- Madonna – 'Material Girl'

- Nas – 'I Can'

- Fergie – 'Glamourous'

- Pink Floyd – 'Money'

- Gwen Stefani – 'Rich Girl'

- Kelis – 'Millionaire'

- Ariana Grande – '7 Rings'

- M.I.A – 'Paper Planes'

- Bruno Mars – 'Billionaire'

There are also loads of songs and subliminals that you can find on YouTube that have positive affirmations around money looping but which have a relaxation sound over them, like a thunderstorm or waves crashing on a beach. These are my go-to for going to sleep, and I leave them playing all through the night. This will allow your subconscious mind to be reprogrammed by the positive affirmations in the subliminal, creating a mindset shift for you!

Month Six

MANIFESTING YOUR DREAM FRIENDSHIPS

The great business philosopher Jim Rohn once said that you are an average of the five people that you spend the most time with. Now, if that doesn't highlight how important it is that we surround ourselves with people we aspire to be like, then I don't know what will! Think of the five people that you spend most of your time with. Would you be happy to essentially be a product of them? Think about the qualities that you want to possess as your highest achieving version of yourself and think about the bad habits that you want to cut out of your life. Do the people around you support this transition, do they possess these qualities, do they participate in these bad habits? Having a team and a good support system around you that believes in you and supports your dreams is so important for living your best life. Even though it is great to be able to stand on your own two feet, and I know a lot of people pride themselves on being independent, but there is nothing better than having a 'home team'. Those people who are there for you no matter the time, no matter how far, no matter the circumstance. We often go through different stages of having different friendships throughout our life. Only a select few are usually around for ever, and this is a good thing. Have you ever felt like you are struggling with a certain friendship group? Or like the conversation of a group of friends no longer interests you and you actually feel bored when you are around them? Or like you have nothing in common with people who you used to spend hours a day talking to? This isn't a bad thing; if anything, it is a good thing, it's a sign that you are growing, evolving, levelling up and moving on to higher things. Although sometimes a drift in a friendship or people cutting you out of their life can be upsetting, remember that, especially once you are starting your law of attraction journey and you are manifesting your dream life, the Universe may remove people from your life who are blocking you from attaining that dream. The Universe hears conversations that you don't and if you are manifesting for happiness and good people around you, then the Universe will find a way to declutter the negative vibes. If manifesting closer friendships or a better quality of relationship with your current friends is something you want to focus on, first of all we need to do some self-reflection work and figure out how happy and content we are with our friendships in our life. This month your journal task will be to do some self-reflection around how your friendships have changed over time, what sort of a friend you are, the quality of friendships that you have in your life and your ideal friendship goals.

Journal prompts for figuring out your friendship goals

1. What qualities do you look for in your friends?

2. What is an ideal friend to you?

3. Think of your closest friends right now. Where did you meet them? How did your friendship form?

4. What is your perfect thing to do when you hang out with a friend?

5. Have you ever struggled with maintaining friendships? Why is this? Document all the times you have lost a friend and see if there is any pattern, and how can you change this.

6. When was the last time you showed kindness to a friend? How did this make them feel? And how did it make you feel? How will you show a friend kindness this week?

7. Do you believe in quality over quantity when it comes to friendship?

8. How important are friends to you, and how have they influenced you?

9. What does 'friendship' mean to you?

10. Write a thank you letter to your best friend, and detail all the things that you are grateful for about them, and then you can even post this to them.

11. What kind of advice would you offer a younger version of yourself regarding friends?

12. Identify a relationship you have that serves no purpose at all. Is there anything negative keeping you stuck in this pattern?

13. Name the three people who, if you were in trouble and needed them right now, would be there for you. Do you count these people as close friends?

14. If you could create the perfect social circle, what sort of people would you want in your group? What conversations would you want to have?

15. Write about friendships that ended on a bad note. How did this experience affect you? Did anyone's action hurt you? Did your actions hurt anyone?

16. How do people who have just met you describe you? What feedback do you often get?

17. How would your close friends describe you? Would you say this is an accurate description? And how does this make you feel?

18. Write about a time that you felt lonely and isolated. What did you do to pull yourself out of this state?

19. What sort of person brings out the best in you and makes you feel most comfortable?

20. What sort of people do you attract? What are a lot of your friendships built upon? Where did you meet them?

21. Choose three goals that are important to you personally. Who have you told these goals to? If nobody, why? What would their reaction be? Detail it.

22. Write down the name of your first best friend from primary school. How old were you when you met? Do you keep in contact with them? How has their life changed over the years? Are you in two totally different spaces now? How is your life different to theirs?

23. Do you count on your friends or your family more?

24. Think about a time where you have had to put a friend's needs above yours and be completely selfless. How did this make you feel?

25. Think about your relationships now. In what ways do they differ from those created years ago?

Manifesting your dream friendships using visualisation

So, this month we will be focusing all our visualisation exercises on manifesting good, healthy friendships that make us feel fulfilled. Now we have done our journaling around friendships, we should have a clearer vision of what friendship means to us and what our core values are. First of all, you can use your visual aid: your vision board. Add pictures of the type of friendship group you would like to have. You could use fictional friendship groups. For example, if you would like a mixed-gender group of friends, you could add a picture of the cast of *Friends*; if you would like just one best friend you could add a picture of Serena van der Woodsen and Blair Waldorf from *Gossip Girl*, or any other fictional friendships that you aspire to have. If you currently have good friendships in your life, then you may want to attach some pictures of trips that you would like to take or places that you would like to visit together. You could also write on your vision board qualities that you value in a friendship that you want to attract into your life. Remember when you place the pictures on your board to think positive thoughts about these friendship manifestations. Put out that good energy into the Universe, then let go and trust that the Universe is bringing these high-vibes relationships into your life.

Another method that you can use to visualise an ideal friendship is the cinema method. The best time to use the cinema method is for twenty minutes before you go to bed or for twenty minutes after you wake up, when the subconscious mind is most active. Then I want you to vividly visualise where it is that you want to go in terms of your friendship goals. For example, if you are manifesting that an old friend re-enters your life, you should first visualise all the good times that you and that person shared and really feel grateful for all of them. Next imagine you and that person having the conversation where you speak about why it is that you are not talking any more. Imagine where this conversation is taking place. Is it at a place where you two used to spend time a lot? Visualise that you are getting to say your side of what happened, and how you feel about things; you get to apologise, and you express how much you have missed them. Imagine that the other person listens to you, sees where you are coming from, apologises too and says that they have missed you as well. Then I want you to go on to visualise all the things that you two enjoy doing in your spare time with each other. Imagine telling the rest of your friends that you two have made peace and imagine you are all happy, thriving and spending quality time together again. Ensure that you are sending out to the Universe positive vibrations around this relationship, showing gratitude for this person, and then trust that the Universe will tune into your frequency and deliver you your desire, as it always does. If you are trying to manifest a new group of friends into your life, you will need to think about the qualities and the morals that you want them to possess. It may be hard to visualise what they look like without having met them yet, so if you are struggling with that, think of a fictional character, think about how their qualities might affect your friendship, think about whether they are the person you call when you are in need, think about the laughter you two will share, think about the activities you would like to do with someone who has the qualities that you are looking for in a best friend, and think about how happy this would make you feel!

Manifesting your dream friendships using positive affirmations

This month we are going to focus our positive affirmations on manifesting good friendships into our life, and you can do this however suits you. If you have been saying your affirmations every morning while getting ready, this month why don't you voice record yourself saying them on repeat and play them to yourself while commuting to work or doing a workout, whatever floats your boat! I have selected some positive affirmations that you can use this month to manifest your ideal friendship; however, as always, please do tweak and adjust them to suit you.

1. People enjoy being friends with me.

2. I attract friends that possess [*list qualities*] into my life.

3. My friendship is an important part of my life.

4. I choose to only surround myself with healthy friendships.

5. All my friends are focused on creating a better life for themselves, just like I am.

6. I have a positive vibe that attracts a positive tribe.

7. I welcome new like-minded people into my life.

8. I love and accept myself, and I am a magnet for good friends.

9. I can imagine all the great things me and my friend are going to do together.

10. All of my friendships are real, loyal and genuine.

11. I am creating long-lasting friendships by always being there for my friends.

12. Me and my friends share common interests, and we always have something to talk about.

13. My friends support my dreams and aspirations and I support theirs.

14. My friend is my biggest fan, and I am theirs.

15. My inner circle only consists of good, kind people.

16. I don't chase. I attract. What is meant for me will find me.

17. Every day I am open to meeting new friends.

18. I remove all negative people from my life, with no bad blood.

19. My old friend [*say name*] will reach out and we will make amends.

20. Good people enter my life all the time.

21. I know my best friend will appear in my life at a perfect time.

22. I make the effort to be a good and supportive friend.

23. I love my friends even though they aren't perfect and neither am I.

24. I am my real self when I am with my friends and there is no judgement there.

25. I find joy in being a good friend to the people that I love.

Manifesting your dream friendships using scripting

For my queens who love the scripting method, this month we are of course going to be focusing on our scripts to manifest the ideal friendships into our life. One of the activities that you can do is write a journal entry and date it with the last day of this month. I want you to start the diary entry with 'I have had amazing, fulfilling friendships this month.' Then go on to create a list and title it 'the qualities of the closest five people around me' and detail all of the qualities you want to manifest in your ideal friends. Then create another list titled 'what me and my friends like to do in our spare time' and detail the activities. Then detail how grateful you feel and why about the friends you have in your life. Maybe they are always there when you need them? Maybe they always lift you up when you are feeling down? Maybe they are always up for doing one of your favourite activities with you? Whatever it is that you look for in a best friend, be sure to write it out and be as specific as possible.

Using the 3-3-3 or 5-5-5 method

You can use the 3-3-3 or the 5-5-5 method to script the life that you want. Now, people often ask which one is the better one for them to use and, honestly, it is just whatever one that you feel more comfortable with and have the most time to do. So what you need to do is choose one of the positive affirmations from the previous page, and if you are doing the 3-3-3 method then you are going to write this 33 times for 3 days, and if you are using the 5-5-5 method then you are going to write this 55 times for 5 days. Now, as always, just putting pen to paper won't bring your manifestations to you; you need to put out the high-vibrational energy around your manifestation, so that the Universe can tune into this frequency and deliver. So, before you do this practice, ensure you have a high vibe, by using gratitude and doing activities that make you feel good. Then once you have performed the 3-3-3 or 5-5-5 method, ensure you let go and trust that the Universe is bringing your manifestation to you, like it always does!

Using the 3-6-9 method

Lastly, queens, you can use the 3-6-9 method. All of you will have different ideas of how you can achieve satisfaction in this month's area; it may be a new friend, doing fun things with current friends, or making up with a past friend. Try to use the 3-6-9 method every day, if possible, to focus on your intention and put it out into the Universe. First write the 'thing' that you want 3 times, then the action related to the thing as if it has already happened, and repeat this 6 times, and lastly the emotion connected to your manifestation 9 times. I will give you an example that you can use below:

Amazing friendship group

Amazing friendship group

Amazing friendship group

I have an amazing friendship group, whose values are aligned with mine and who are focused on achieving the finer things in life like I am.

Manifesting Your Dream Friendships

*I have an amazing friendship group, whose values
are aligned with mine and who are focused on
achieving the finer things in life like I am.*

*I have an amazing friendship group, whose values
are aligned with mine and who are focused on
achieving the finer things in life like I am.*

*I have an amazing friendship group, whose values
are aligned with mine and who are focused on
achieving the finer things in life like I am.*

*I have an amazing friendship group, whose values
are aligned with mine and who are focused on
achieving the finer things in life like I am.*

*I have an amazing friendship group, whose values
are aligned with mine and who are focused on
achieving the finer things in life like I am.*

*I have an amazing friendship group, whose values
are aligned with mine and who are focused on
achieving the finer things in life like I am.
I am so grateful and content.*

*I have an amazing friendship group, whose values
are aligned with mine and who are focused on
achieving the finer things in life like I am.
I am so grateful and content.*

I have an amazing friendship group, whose values are aligned with mine and who are focused on achieving the finer things in life like I am. I am so grateful and content.

I have an amazing friendship group, whose values are aligned with mine and who are focused on achieving the finer things in life like I am. I am so grateful and content.

I have an amazing friendship group, whose values are aligned with mine and who are focused on achieving the finer things in life like I am. I am so grateful and content.

I have an amazing friendship group, whose values are aligned with mine and who are focused on achieving the finer things in life like I am. I am so grateful and content.

I have an amazing friendship group, whose values are aligned with mine and who are focused on achieving the finer things in life like I am. I am so grateful and content.

I have an amazing friendship group, whose values are aligned with mine and who are focused on achieving the finer things in life like I am. I am so grateful and content.

*I have an amazing friendship group, whose values
are aligned with mine and who are focused on
achieving the finer things in life like I am.
I am so grateful and content.*

Month Seven

MANIFESTING GOOD HEALTH

This month we are going to be focusing on manifesting good health. How many of you take your health for granted? We all know that feeling when we get a cold, and we have a blocked nose and a sore throat and we say, 'I can't remember how it feels to be able to breathe normally or swallow without it feeling like I am swallowing broken glass!' We promise in that moment to never take our health for granted again. But guess what . . . as soon as we are back to normal, we forget what it felt like to be ill and we take advantage of our health again. Most of us probably take it for granted that we have all five of our senses working without any aid, and we are able to see, to hear, to touch, to smell, to taste. Imagine how different your life would be if even one of your senses stopped working! We would miss the small things, like hearing the birds in the morning, seeing the face of our loved one, the smell of freshly cut grass, or that first sip of your morning coffee – the simple things in life that we sometimes forget are so special. Do you ever wake up in the morning and thank the Universe for another day, or do you wake up and snooze the dreaded alarm, moan that you can't be bothered with the hustle and bustle of the morning commute, and moan that you are tired! I know that I am guilty of this, but imagine if one day we woke up and our poor health stopped us from ever returning to what we see as normal again. All our so-called struggles that we think we face every day would in fact seem like minor issues. You know what they say, health really is your wealth! Health is something that a lot of us neglect, until it suddenly goes wrong for us or somebody that we know. So, start today. Recognise your bad habits that could be cutting years off your life, and implement new ones. Reflect on how you have been living, and think of the better life choices that you could make. Think of where you would like to see yourself in twenty years' time, and if you carry on the way you are living, will that be likely? Without good health we will not be able to achieve all our dreams and desires; our body is the most powerful instrument that we own and we must care for it and treat it with the respect that it deserves! Our bodies are so advanced. Just think about the process of how a life comes into this world: the moment of conception, the growth of the baby and then the birth; it is just incredible! Think about all the systems in our bodies: the respiratory system that allows us to breathe without having to think about it; the cardiovascular system that allows blood to circulate;

the digestive system that allows us to process all the food that we eat; the endocrine system that produces all our hormones; the urinary system that allows us to get rid of waste; the reproductive system, which allows the human race to carry on; the nervous system that allows all of the body systems to communicate – amazing!

Now, although our physical health is extremely important, so is our mental health. Our mental health dictates how we think, feel and act. It is important to take care of our mental health to reduce anxiety, increase our self-esteem, improve our relationships, make better decisions, and improve the way that we feel. It is completely normal to have days where you don't feel like getting out of bed, but if you feel like this most of the time, please remember how important it is to seek support from someone and express how you feel to a doctor, a friend or a family member, because talking can give us hope and reassure us that it can be okay not to be okay. There are so many factors that can affect our mental health, such as finances, the weather, the food we eat, other people and our genes. Poor mental health can lead to us missing out on things in life; we can lose friends, jobs, housing and control of our own life. So, it is important to recognise when you're struggling and to reach out for help. Before we go on to setting our goals for the month, we need to do some self-reflection on where we feel like we are physically and mentally. We will do this by doing our journaling for this month's topic: health. I have listed out some journal prompts to get you going below:

Journal prompts for figuring out your physical health goals

1. What feature of your body are you most grateful for? Detail why.

2. Think about the ways that your senses help you to enjoy your life. List the five senses and write next to each of them some of the things that they enable you to enjoy.

3. Throughout your life, when have you felt the healthiest and what weight were you? What were you doing different then compared to now? Can you get back into that lifestyle?

4. When do you feel the most energised?

5. Would you say that you have a balanced diet?

6. Were you considered a 'sporty' child? Did you have any hobbies that involved exercise?

7. How do you feel about exercise? How does it make you feel?

8. What is your favourite sport to play that gets you moving? If you don't have one then what did you enjoy the most at school?

9. What are some ways to make exercise even more fun?

10. Is there anyone that you could make your fitness buddy so you can hold each other accountable for working out? Reach out to them and get a plan in place.

11. How does your body feel after you exercise? And how does your mind feel? Does it feel a lot clearer?

12. What time of the day do you like to exercise?

13. What is something you are doing right now to pursue good health?

14. What is a bad habit that you should stop doing right now for your health and wellbeing?

15. How old will you be in fifteen years? How do you want your physical health to be then? How do you want your body to work? How do you want to be walking around?

16. Write a note for your future self to read when you are not feeling well. What are some things that healthy you would tell yourself to make yourself feel better?

17. What healthy habits do you want to build?

18. What is your body trying to tell you?

19. What manageable health goal do you want to set for yourself this week?

20. Has there ever been a time you have set a fitness goal and achieved it? How did this make you feel?

21. Write a letter to your body.

22. What are your body's warning signs? When do you know you are burnt out?

23. Do you drink enough water?

24. Do you eat five a day?

25. Do you incorporate enough vegetables into your meals?

Journal prompts for figuring out your mental health goals

1. Talk about your day.

2. What are ten things that you are grateful for today?

3. List and describe your emotions.

4. What do you like most about your personality?

5. Do you struggle to say no to things? What boundaries could you put in place to change this?

6. Write a letter of forgiveness to yourself.

7. What is your favourite part of the day?

8. List three things that you are currently stressed about, now go through this list and question whether you have the ability to change any of these.

9. Is your anxiety tied to a memory or experience? If so, detail it here; it's a safe place.

10. Is there anybody in your life that you can talk to who understands and can relate to your anxiety disorder?

11. If you could write a letter to any of your fears, which would it be? Write this letter now.

12. When you have bad anxiety, write how you feel, then count backwards from 100, and again write how you feel different afterwards.

13. Make ten promises to yourself and detail each one.

14. Write down some songs that always cheer you up, then turn them into a playlist.

15. In what areas of your life do you feel like you need to spend more time and energy?

16. Is your anxiety worse out or at home?

17. How is your stress affecting your physical health?

18. Do you have trouble sleeping? If so, what habits are hindering your sleep?

19. What healthy habits for your mental health can you start incorporating more often?

20. What are some things that you say no to because of your mental health? What are some things that you want to say yes to?

21. How do you feel you could have more peace in your life?

22. What has been your biggest lesson so far in your mental health journey?

23. What or who inspires you the most?

24. What motivates you when you have extreme anxiety?

25. Anxiety isn't always a bad thing. What are some of the ways it might have helped you?

Manifesting good health using visualisation

As we are all different, all of our health goals will be totally different too, and I am going to give you examples of different ways you can manifest these health goals. If you are trying to manifest a dream body weight or a type of figure, then you could print off images online, or if it is a weight-loss goal to get to a weight you used to be before, then you can print off old pictures of yourself when you were that body weight! You could also create a visual aid by printing off a picture of blank scales and writing down your ideal weight in there. Then you could add pictures of how you plan to lose this weight or gain the muscle. For example, if you plan to wake up early every morning and go to the gym before work, you could print off a picture of an alarm clock with the time you want to get up, of the healthy meals you will be eating and the exercises that you will be carrying out. This will allow your routine to be prominent in your mind and motivate you every time you see your vision board to keep working towards your goals. You could also add motivational quotes around your fitness section of your vision board to motivate you even further. If you are trying to manifest stopping smoking or vaping, you could work out how much you would save over a twelve-month period on average, and print off a cheque with this figure on it to motivate you each time you go to cave in to your addiction. You could also post a picture of healthy lungs. If you have a goal of being able to run, swim or cycle a certain distance, then you could print out a picture of a map and outline how far this distance would be, and you could also print off a picture of you doing the activity as a reminder of how much you enjoy it and to give you a confidence boost that you can do it. When you are putting these images on the board, it is important that you believe in yourselve that you can do it, and that you've got rid of any limiting beliefs, and be in a high vibration. Then every time you see these images, be sure to radiate so much positive energy to the Universe about them.

If you are focusing on manifesting your ideal mental health, however, then you could post images of things that make you happy or that have connotations with being happy, such as sunshine, laughter, cuddles, good food or spending time with family. You could also post pictures of people in your life that make you feel happy, such as a family member or friends. You could even write quotes that inspire you to be happy, and positive words such as 'content' or 'abundance'.

If you want to use the cinema method to visualise good health, then you need to do this for twenty minutes after you wake up or for twenty minutes before you go to bed, as this is when the subconscious mind is most active. Visualise that on the screen you can see your ideal self at your optimum health. If you want to manifest weight loss or a change in fitness, think about what you look like, have you changed body shape? Have you changed the way you dress? Are you more confident? Are more people giving you compliments? If so, what are the compliments and how do they make you feel? Visualise yourself standing on the scales and seeing your target goal, visualise yourself doing the exercise you want to be able to do without being too out of breath, imagine yourself finally being able to do it and imagine how proud of yourself you feel! Has your daily routine changed, do you wake up early feeling great, and get ready and drive to the gym? Imagine every single step from getting ready to finishing your work-out and be as specific as you can. If you are trying to manifest running a marathon, visualise applying for the marathon and getting that letter through the door to say you have been accepted and how happy you are! Visualise the training, think about who you are doing it with and who gives you support. Think about what you wear to training, the struggles you are faced with but overcome. Visualise crossing that line, who will be there to cheer you on, imagine holding up that medal, imagine the joy on everyone's faces, and imagine that bath as soon as you get home, where you can lay back, relax and know that you made it. If you currently have poor health and are trying to manifest your recovery, think about what the first thing is you will do once you are better, who you will tell, where you will go and who you will be with. Be really specific and as real as possible. And, as always, be sure to let go and let the Universe bring your manifestations to fruition.

Manifesting good health using positive affirmations

Here are some positive affirmations that you can use this month to manifest good health. I would recommend choosing a few specific affirmations to focus on saying repeatedly daily.

1. I am strong and healthy.

2. Every cell in my body knows what to do to keep me healthy and fit.

3. I willingly commit my energy to ensure good health.

4. I am in love with my body, mind and soul.

5. I send love to all the organs in my body for keeping me healthy and strong.

6. My body is sacred and I will take care of it.

7. My body is always working for me.

8. My immune system is strong and keeps me safe.

9. I deserve to live a long and healthy life

10. Self-care means eating healthily, exercising, and getting enough rest.

11. I am grateful for the good health the Universe has given to me.

12. I am capable of controlling my cravings.

13. I am losing weight to be healthier, look better and feel happier.

14. I commit myself to work on my health and fitness every day.

15. I surround myself with people who love and support me.

16. I am worthy of a healthy body and mind.

17. I am filled with strength.

18. My body is a vessel for calm energy.

19. I do not carry stress or tension in my body.

20. I do not carry any stress in my body.

21. I am grateful for my life.

22. I can do anything that I put my mind to.

23. Anxiety does not rule my life.

24. I am enough. I have enough.

25. I allow myself to be me.

Manifesting good health using scripting

You can use the 3-6-9 method to manifest good health into your life. As all of you will have different goals, you will need to write the 'thing' that you want to manifest down 3 times, then write down the action related to the thing 6 times and then lastly the emotion that you will feel once you receive the thing 9 times. An example of how you would lay this out for weight loss or for anxiety is written below:

2 stone / calm

2 stone / calm

2 stone / calm

I have lost 2 stone through hard work and determination /
I am now so much calmer in my life and rarely
have anxiety.

*I have lost 2 stone through hard work and determination /
I am now so much calmer in my life and rarely
have anxiety.*

*I have lost 2 stone through hard work and determination /
I am now so much calmer in my life and rarely
have anxiety.*

*I have lost 2 stone through hard work and determination /
I am now so much calmer in my life and rarely
have anxiety.*

*I have lost 2 stone through hard work and determination /
I am now so much calmer in my life and rarely
have anxiety.*

*I have lost 2 stone through hard work and determination /
I am now so much calmer in my life and rarely
have anxiety.*

*I have lost 2 stone through hard work and determination
and I feel confident and proud /
I am now so much calmer in my life and rarely have
anxiety, and this makes me feel confident.*

*I have lost 2 stone through hard work and determination
and I feel confident and proud /
I am now so much calmer in my life and rarely have
anxiety, and this makes me feel confident.*

*I have lost 2 stone through hard work and determination
and I feel confident and proud /
I am now so much calmer in my life and rarely have
anxiety, and this makes me feel confident.*

*I have lost 2 stone through hard work and determination
and I feel confident and proud /
I am now so much calmer in my life and rarely have
anxiety, and this makes me feel confident.*

*I have lost 2 stone through hard work and determination
and I feel confident and proud /
I am now so much calmer in my life and rarely have
anxiety, and this makes me feel confident.*

*I have lost 2 stone through hard work and determination
and I feel confident and proud /
I am now so much calmer in my life and rarely have
anxiety, this makes me feel confident.*

*I have lost 2 stone through hard work and determination
and I feel confident and proud /
I am now so much more calmer in my life and rarely have
anxiety, and this makes me feel confident.*

*I have lost 2 stone through hard work and determination
and I feel confident and proud /
I am now so much calmer in my life and rarely have
anxiety, and this makes me feel confident.*

*I have lost 2 stone through hard work and determination
and I feel confident and proud /
I am now so much calmer in my life and rarely have
anxiety, and this makes me feel confident.*

Try to do this every day, if possible. Once you have finished this practice, is it important that you breathe in, breathe out and let go.

Another scripting exercise that you can do is write down all the things that you are currently grateful for in your life in regard to your physical health. This could be as simple as being grateful for your taste buds that allow you to taste your breakfast every morning or your legs that work perfectly to help you move about. Then I want you to write down everything that you want to manifest about your physical health as if you already have it and are grateful for it. For example, if you are trying to manifest an increase in your fitness levels, you would write: 'I am grateful for having high fitness levels.' A scripting exercise that you can do for your mental health is to write down all the common negative phrases that come out of your mouth, for example: 'I am so depressed and down.' Then write next to each one a replacement positive phrase you are going to say each time you have this thought, like: 'I am so grateful for another day on this earth, I am lucky to be alive.' This way you are making a mental note that each time you go to say something negative with a low vibe that you need to replace it with something positive.

You can also use the 3-3-3 or the 5-5-5 method, which-ever one you prefer, and choose one of your positive affirmations around health and write this down 33 times for 3 days or 55 times for 5 days!

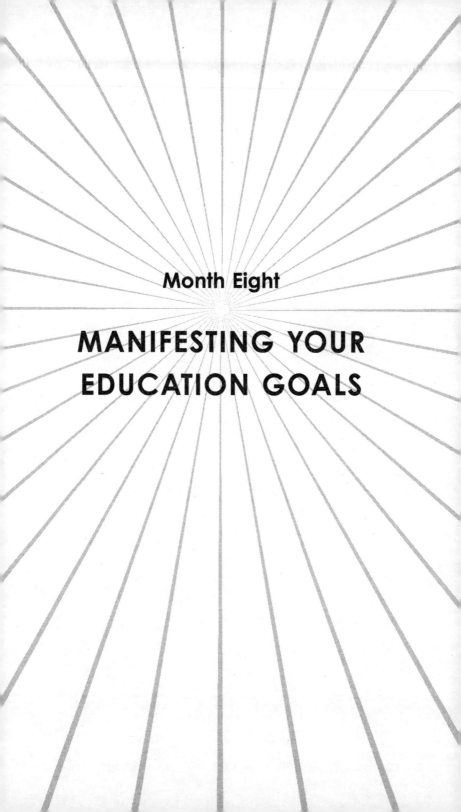

Month Eight

MANIFESTING YOUR EDUCATION GOALS

When you read the word 'education', what comes to mind for you? Do you see education as a good thing, or does it take you back to your days in school where you couldn't wait to leave? Education isn't just the act of learning new information, it is also about sharing your knowledge with others. There are many benefits to education; for example, it can open doors to new job opportunities and it can also help you in gaining a higher income. Have you ever been in the situation where you are doing the same job as someone else, and maybe even a better job than them, but because they have a qualification, they are earning more than you? Being in education and completing a course and getting a title or a certificate at the end of it can give you a huge sense of achievement and help to boost your confidence and make you feel like you could take on anything! When was the last time that you participated in any form of education? Was it in high school or college? Or have you gone on to complete courses and exams for your career? Have you ever been put off carrying on education because you fear failure or because of the financial sacrifice? Well, good news for you, manifesting queens: you can use the law of attraction, along with a bit of hard work, to manifest your educational desires.

If you are currently in education and you have exams coming up, are you one of those people that spend more time stressing over the outcome of the exam rather than actually being productive with your time preparing for it? I was one of those people until I started to make revision plans. A revision plan is the stepping stone between where you are now and the outcome you desire; it helps you to stay productive and motivated but also helps ease your nerves when you realise just how much you can get done in the time you have. I want you to write down the grade you desire. Don't be scared of aiming too high, just put pen to paper and write it down. By doing this you are already manifesting it, you are putting out into the Universe what you want. To create a revision plan, first obtain a breakdown of every area or topic you need to know about in order to get your grade. Go through this list and rate them by how much time you will need to spend on them to how little time you will need to spend on them, and you could colour code this with red, amber and green. Then, in an Excel spreadsheet, create a seven-day-week table, and input the hours that you will be studying into this table. Finally, allocate the topics you're studying to your time slots. This revision plan doesn't need to be definite, and there is no need to panic if you do not stick to it religiously, but it is good to use as a guide, as it keeps you motivated and gives you an overview of how much you have done and how much you have left to do.

Another way that you can reduce your stress for exams, is to ensure that you start studying as early as you can. This will give you enough days and hours in your revision plan to cover everything and revisit areas that you are unsure of. Making sure that you get enough sleep, taking regular breaks for exercise, even if it is just a walk round the block, buying yourself new stationery that motivates you to want to revise and eating brain foods such as bananas and blueberries will all increase your wellbeing when taking exams and will help you to cope with the stress in a more effective way. There are loads of ways that you can revise, such as note-taking, cue cards, spider diagrams or making visual notes; however, just because one method works for someone else doesn't mean that it will work for you, or just because one method works for you in one subject doesn't mean that it will work for you in another subject. A good place to start would be find-ing out what type of learner you are: the visual learning style means you learn by observing and analysing things, such as pictures or graphs; with the auditory learning style, you learn best through sounds, such as listening to things being explained on a video or in a lecture; the next learning style is the reading and writing style, where you learn by reading textbooks and writing; the last style of learning is the kinaesthetic learning style, which is where you learn by doing things and talking out loud. You can take a test by by searching online for The Vark Questionnaire.* Once you find out what type of learner you are, you can start to use the appropriate methods to help you take in more information and learn more effectively!

But before we can manifest our goals in education, we need to do some self-reflection around our perception of education and find out what it is that we really want. We will do this using journaling and I have added some journal prompts to help you below.

Journal prompts for figuring out your education goals

1. How did you find school as a child?

2. Did you get good grades at school? If so, were you praised? If you didn't, were you punished? How did this make you feel?

3. Would you say you are intelligent? Describe why?

4. What was your favourite subject at school and why?

5. At what age did you leave school? What did you go on to do?

---

* https://vark-learn.com/the-vark-questionnaire/

6. If you didn't need a qualification to do any career, what would you go into and why? Is it different to what you are doing now?

7. Is there a qualification that is in between you and a promotion at work? If so, why have you not gone for it? Is it a money stress? Is it the fear of failure? Is there a way that you could resolve this?

8. What is your first memory of failing? How did this make you feel?

9. What have you learnt from past failures? Have you used them to grow? If not, how can you use them to better yourself?

10. Are there any free courses or training that appeal to you, that you could take alongside work to give you another skill? If so, what is stopping you from pursuing this? Do you blame time a lot? Think of one thing you could stop doing to give yourself a free hour a week to work on yourself.

11. Do you think education has shaped the person you are? Why?

12. What do you wish had been taught to you at school, and is it something that you know a lot about now? Or is it something that you can do a course in?

13. What is one thing you want to ensure your kids are educated about that isn't included in the school

curriculum? Do you have enough knowledge about this topic to pass on to your kids? If not, why? What actions are you going to take to ensure you know more about this topic?

14. Do you think the education system is fair?

15. Do you think people born into money become more successful because they have more resources? If so, why? Do you take advantage of all the free services accessible to you, such as YouTube, the internet and the library?

16. Did you go to university? If you did, was it worth it? If you didn't, what was stopping you?

17. If you never went to university, would you like to now? Is there any stigma stopping you? Please detail your thinking.

18. Do you ever feel envious of other people's educational achievements? If so, why? What triggers this?

19. What leaders do you find inspirational and why? Has education helped them get there?

20. What excuses do you commonly find yourself using as to why you have not achieved your educational goals? List these excuses, and now think of a plan as to how you can solve them.

21. Do you think education gives you power?

22. Do you see education as a stepping stone to earning more money, or to developing yourself as a person?

23. Do you feel like you pass on your knowledge to people as much as you should? If not, why?

24. What soft skills have you acquired?

25. List down five things that you are good at that you could teach to other people.

Manifesting your education goals using visualisation

Whether you are currently in education or if some self-reflection sparked a new goal to go into education and further your knowledge, you can use your vision board as a visual aid to put out to the Universe your dreams and desires and to make them prominent in your mind! First let's talk exam results. You should post a picture on your vision board of the certificate that you would receive and also add in your own name on the certificate. If you are wanting specific grades or an exam result, make sure that you print this off nice and big and post it on there. You could post pictures of the tools you use to revise, such as books and stationery, to keep your focus aligned with your goals and so that every time you see your board you feel motivated and you remember that you need to do your revision in order to reach these desired results. If, for example, you wanted to manifest doing a particular course for work that would enable you to go further in your career or get a pay rise, post pictures of the qualification's logo on there, write yourself a fake certificate and even photoshop a picture of yourself holding it! The possibilities of where you can go on your journey with education are endless, and remember: do not be too scared to dream big when placing your images on your vision board, and manifest that shit, queen!

Another way that you can manifest your education goals if you are trying to manifest a specific exam result is to act out that you are opening your envelope with your results disclosed or logging in to your email to view them, and actually create an email or a letter. Every time you open it I want you to jump up and down with joy and scream about how happy you are! I created a TikTok about how you can use this technique to manifest passing your driving test and my messages went absolutely crazy with people telling me how much it had helped them, even some people who had failed multiple times before!

You can, of course, also use the cinema technique to manifest this when the subconscious part of your brain is most active, which is during the twenty minutes before you go to bed and the first twenty minutes after you wake up. Visualise this moment happening, picture what you're wearing, where you are and who's around you!

You can also use the cinema technique to visualise getting told that work will pay for you to go to university and get a degree, that work will pay for your training or that you have been selected to do a course for free that will help you to gain a new skill.

Manifesting your education goals using positive affirmations

Choose a couple of these positive affirmations to repeat daily each week. You can incorporate these into your daily routine when you are taking a shower, or on your way to work, and you can even record them and play them on a loop to listen to on your commute or while you're working.

1. I have achieved [say result] in my test.

2. I can achieve anything that I put my mind to.

3. I am smart and hardworking and deserve the results that are for me.

4. I thank the Universe for blessing me with my intelligence.

5. I am a fast learner and find it easy to learn new things.

6. I am organised and know what I need to do to achieve my goal.

7. I just sat my [*say the name of the test*] and I found it easy.

8. I smashed all the obstacles in the way of me achieving my goal.

9. There are endless possibilities of what I can achieve.

10. I am in control of my success.

11. Education is a tool that I can use to upgrade my life.

12. I am grateful for every experience that I get to learn.

13. I obtain many skills that I can pass on to other people.

14. I believe that I can be anything that I want to be.

15. Knowledge is power.

16. I am hard-working.

17. I strive for success.

18. Success is my middle name.

19. I am a great teacher.

20. I am worthy of obtaining the [*say qualification*].

21. I enjoy learning.

22. Learning comes easily to me.

23. I allow myself the time I deserve to spend on my education.

24. I have the money to fund my education.

25. I have achieved the education I want for free.

Manifesting your education goals using scripting

You can definitely use the 3-6-9 method to manifest your desired exam results. I have done it multiple times and got either the exact percentage I manifested or I was 2 per cent out either way. I could not believe it the first time that it happened. This month make sure that you do this practice as many times a week as you can remember. First of all you need to write down what you want to manifest 3 times, then you need to write the action to do with the thing you want and you need to write this down 6 times, and lastly you need to write down the emotion connected with the thing you want to manifest and write this down 9 times.

An example of how you could use the 3-6-9 method to manifest your education goals is:

[insert the name of the qualification]

[insert the name of the qualification]

[insert the name of the qualification]

The opportunity for me to gain the [insert the name of the qualification] qualification has come into my life.

The opportunity for me to gain the [insert the name of the qualification] qualification has come into my life.

The opportunity for me to gain the [insert the name of the qualification] qualification has come into my life.

The opportunity for me to gain the [insert the name of the qualification] qualification has come into my life.

The opportunity for me to gain the [insert the name of the qualification] qualification has come into my life.

The opportunity for me to gain the [insert the name of the qualification] qualification has come into my life.

The opportunity for me to gain the [insert the name of the qualification] qualification has come into my life and I feel so privileged.

The opportunity for me to gain the [insert the name of the qualification] qualification has come into my life and I feel so privileged.

The opportunity for me to gain the [insert the name of the qualification] qualification has come into my life and I feel so privileged.

The opportunity for me to gain the [insert the name of the qualification] qualification has come into my life and I feel so privileged.

The opportunity for me to gain the [insert the name of the qualification] qualification has come into my life and I feel so privileged.

The opportunity for me to gain the [insert the name of the qualification] qualification has come into my life and I feel so privileged.

The opportunity for me to gain the [insert the name of the qualification] qualification has come into my life and I feel so privileged.

The opportunity for me to gain the [insert the name of the qualification] qualification has come into my life and I feel so privileged.

The opportunity for me to gain the [insert the name of the qualification] qualification has come into my life and I feel so privileged.

You can also try the second way of doing the 3-6-9 method, if you find it too hard to stay present when doing the usual technique. To do it this way, write down an affirmation of the thing you want with the action and the emotion, for example: 'I have got an A* in my history exam, and I am so proud of myself.' Or you can choose a positive affirmation from the list above. Then you need to write this 3 times in the morning, 6 times at lunchtime and then 9 times in the afternoon, and try to do it every day, if possible. This way you are reminding your subconscious brain multiple times a day of your goal and putting pen to paper and pushing it out there into the Universe. The key is to stay present every single time you do this and allow your vibrational energy to be high and feel as if you have already got these results.

As always, once we finish our practice for the day – you already know it – we have to thank the Universe and let it go!

Another method that you can use to manifest your education goals is, every single time that you tick off a topic on your revision plan, say or write: 'Thank you to me for doing the steps necessary to take me one step closer to my A grade', or to whatever grade or mark that you are manifesting. This is so you are making sure that you are not only telling the Universe what your goals are but you are taking action, and you are appreciating your hard work every time that you take that step closer to your goal.

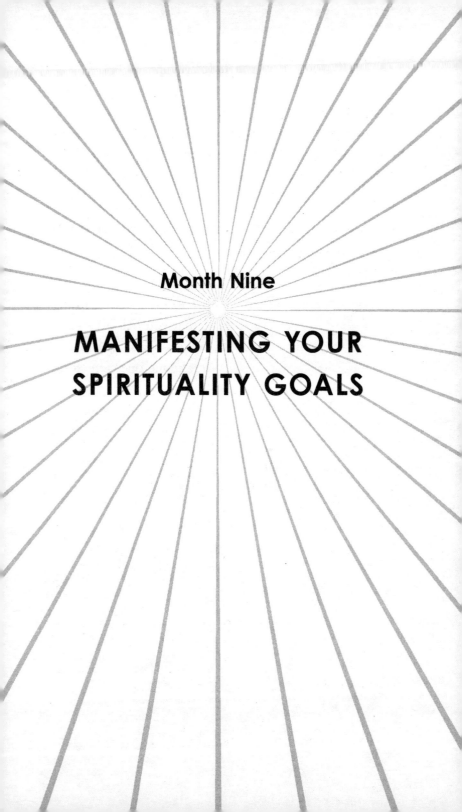

Month Nine

MANIFESTING YOUR SPIRITUALITY GOALS

What does spirituality mean for you? Spirituality can be a feeling that there is something greater than yourself. It can make you feel whole and at peace with every aspect of your life. It can help you to deal with stressful situations and make you feel closer to those around you. Spirituality is a journey, and to some people this starts with a spiritual awakening, which is when you realise you have a higher purpose than what you are doing day to day, like there's something bigger out there for you. Some people can feel like they don't belong in their current life any more. This can seem scary and like something is wrong with you, but it is good, embrace it; you are becoming more at one with yourself and the bigger world around you. If this has never happened to you and you want to invite a spiritual awakening into your life, then there are some steps you can take. The first step is to declutter, getting rid of the old so that you can make room for the new. One time I completely emptied out my room and put my clothes in a bag to donate to charity. I then put these clothes into my car but was too lazy to take them to the charity shop, and because of this I still had an attachment to my old life; I still felt like I was stuck in a rut. Then one day I'd had enough and I donated absolutely everything to charity. It made me feel good that I was helping other people and it made me feel free from my old life, and this was the last straw that needed to happen because my spiritual awakening began. The next step is to start spending more time in nature. I used to walk round a field with my shoes off and feel the grass under my feet and the dirt between my toes. Now, if you have never had a spiritual awakening then this may sound crazy, but there is a lot of energy and spirit outdoors. Another thing that you should do is meditate every morning because it is a great way to clear your head of any negative thoughts and start your day the right way. You can find specific meditations for tapping into your spiritual energy on YouTube. You should be accepting of others. That person at work who you just can't get along with because they have a different way of approaching things to you? Accept them. Your neighbour who always leaves their litter outside no matter how many times you have told them it bothers you? Accept them. Accept people for who they are and know that the only thing that you can control is yourself and the way that you behave. If it bothers you that much then maybe you could take ten minutes out of your day to clean up the front of their house. Not only will this make you feel better, as you will no longer feel irritated by the mess, but it will probably be a great help for them and they will feel grateful towards you. Which brings me on to my next point: giving back and supporting your community. Think of the type of community that you would like to live in. I bet it is a supportive and giving one where everyone helps each other out as opposed to one were everyone is selfish and doesn't talk to one another. If this is the type of community that you want to live in, then be the change, be the one who donates their hand-me-downs to their less fortunate neighbours, who donates to the local food bank, who donates children's toys to the local community. This will make you realise just how lucky you are for the life you lead, even if you don't have a lot, and you'll also feel good about yourself. Another thing that you should do is play high-vibrational music or songs, because how can you feel low if you have music on that is making you feel good? It is impossible to feel two contrasting emotions at once! Another thing that you can do is spare fifteen minutes each morning to practise the 5-5-5 morning routine. This is spending five minutes in the morning meditating or observing your thoughts, five minutes stretching out your body and then five minutes mentally preparing for your day!

This month we are going to tap into our spirituality, and if you try consistently to implement these habits into your life, then I am sure you will see a huge shift. Before we set our goals for how we are going to get in tune with our spiritual side, I want you to do some journaling this month using the journal prompts below. Journaling is also a great way to enhance your spiritual side, as you are doing a lot of self-realisation and finding out more about yourself along the way.

Journal prompts for figuring out your spiritual goals

1. How can you be better person tomorrow than the person that you are today?

2. What emotions do you try to avoid?

3. What words would you use to describe your current relationship with a higher power?

4. How would you describe your ideal relationship with a higher power?

5. Who or what is God to you? How would you describe this higher power?

6. Write about a time when you experienced the Universe's unconditional love.

7. Who is your highest self? How do you align with your highest self in your daily life?

8. What is your purpose on this earth? Do you feel connected with your purpose? If not, what steps can you take to figure out what this is?

9. What blessing are you experiencing in your life right now?

10. What does it mean to you to be connected to all living beings (people, animals, plants, the earth)?

11. Is it possible that you are afraid of spending time alone?

12. Share a time when you felt like God was present with you or spoke to you?

13. What are your three biggest sources of negativity?

14. What do you believe makes the world a better place?

15. Do you believe in coincidences?

16. Where do you see yourself in a year's time? Three years' time and five years' time?

17. When was the last time you met someone new that you had a connection with?

18. Do you compare yourself to anyone? Are you jealous? Why?

19. If you've made mistakes that you still regret to this day, what did you learn from them?

20. How do you practise self-care?

21. What do you want to be remembered for?

22. What types of things do you find annoying?

23. Set a three-minute timer and write whatever comes to mind.

24. Describe one toxic habit that you have and need to let go of.

25. In what areas of your life would you like to see change or growth?

Now we have done some deeper work into finding out more about our true self, we are going to think about the ways that we can become more in tune with our spiritual side. Do you ever sit and think that you have so many good things in your life yet you still don't feel happy? Or are you trying your best to be healthy and exercise and have a new diet, but you still don't seem confident? This is because you are not in touch with your true self. Once you are in touch with your true self, your body will highlight to you what you need, and your actions will be a response to that.

Manifesting your spirituality goals using positive affirmations

Choose a couple of these positive affirmations to repeat daily each week. You can incorporate these into your daily routine when you are taking a shower, or on your way to work, and you can even record them and play them on a loop to listen to on your commute or while working.

1. Everything in life happens for a reason.

2. I am part of the Universe, and the Universe is a part of me.

3. I believe that we're all guided by a divine providence.

4. My spirit is filled with love and compassion.

5. The Universe is always guiding me.

6. I choose to see my difficulties as opportunities to grow closer to a higher power.

7. All is well in my world, as it should be.

8. I trust my inner guidance 100 per cent.

9. I am connected to the wisdom of the Universe.

10. I am a loving soul in a human body.

11. I am acting on my intuition.

12. I am guided by my good feelings.

13. I am aligned with my purpose and truth.

14. I don't chase, I attract. What is meant for me will find me.

15. All that I seek I can find within me.

16. Everything is unfolding in perfect timing. I trust. I believe. I receive.

17. My soul is beautiful.

18. I am loved by the Universe.

19. I am a magnet for miracles.

20. I am a channel for inspiration.

21. Obstacles are opportunities for me to grow.

22. I always let love lead the way.

23. I let go of all limiting beliefs.

24. I release all blocks between me and my dreams.

25. I am an extension of the Universe.

Month Ten

MANIFESTING YOUR DREAM HOME

Now, every single person who is reading this will have a different vision of what 'dream home' means to them. For some of you it may be a huge house where you can grow a family and have room for all your kids; for others it may be renting a room so you can finally get away from home and have your own space. Whatever it is to you, we will be focusing our inner energy on manifesting it this month. So first of all you need to figure out what your style is. How are you going to decorate your dream home? I absolutely love looking on Pinterest for inspiration, so what I want you to do is browse through Pinterest, make a pin board and label it 'I am so grateful for my dream home' – because you know what us manifesting queens are like with our affirmations! Even if the decor on there is for a huge mansion, and you are only manifesting a room to rent, still try to figure out the colours and the style of furniture that you like. Then what you should do is decorate the space you have now with this colour and style of furniture so that every day you are living in alignment with your goals and are constantly surrounded by your manifestation. You are also telling the Universe that you are living out your dream already, meaning it will mirror and reflect this into your life. Next you need to figure out what features you want this home to have, and you need to think of the why. For example, 'I would love a garden, so that in the future when I have kids they can enjoy playing outside' or ' I would like an office, so that I can work on my side hustle in there in peace and have my own space to concentrate'. Think of this as your order to the Universe and keep this safe because we will use it later in the month. Now think about how many rooms you would like to have in your ideal home, think about who would be living there and how long you will be there for and what these rooms will be used for. Now think about the area. At this moment in time these are our dreams and desires and, as you know, we do not hold back, so at the moment we are not thinking about any restrictions and we are not letting our limiting beliefs get in our way! Once we have a rough idea of what we are looking for, it is time to do your homework, so get on Rightmove or similar websites and type in your dream home – the number of bedrooms, the location and so on – and see what comes up. Look at the features and the ones that don't have what you are looking for, cross them off your list! Bookmark the ones that tick all your boxes and we will come back to them later this month.

Now you have actually found houses that are similar to your dream houses, without thinking too much about the finances, ring up the estate agents and go and view them. This will help you to get a feel for the house and allow you to imagine how you would feel once you live there. Now, of course, a house costs money, and what you need to do even if your financial position is a long way off from being able to afford your dream house, is book a free appointment with a mortgage broker, tell them your situation, and see if they can offer any advice or any schemes that can help you. This will give you an idea about how far away your financial situation is from being able to buy your dream home. This should begin to get the ball rolling in your head, and if you are open to it, you will start getting creative and thinking of ways that you can make it possible. Now you know how much you need to save for a deposit, make a spreadsheet of your incomings and your outgoings. Incomings would be your salary and any other income that you receive each month, and outgoings would be all your costs that come out each month: rent, insurance, petrol, food shop, phone bills, credit card payments, loans and so on. Then work out how much you have left each month. How much can you put away? Take into account things like clothes and nights out. Then calculate that if you are saving this much a month, how many months and years will it take you to save for your deposit? Think about any unnecessary outgoings that you can get rid of or reduce, for example by changing providers, and also think about how, if you increased you incomings by say £200 a month, how that could reduce your time frame in saving for this deposit. Now set an amount to increase your income by each month and write it down. By going through all these steps you are literally setting a goal and putting it out to the Universe, and that is how all things begin: a thought, that becomes an idea and then a goal once written down. So even by just writing it down you are getting the ball rolling, allowing your manifestation to start to come to you, and the Universe will bring you opportunities to make this into money. This opportunity may be something like participating in surveys for money, tax rebates, random gifts of money, extra hours at work, or a side hustle idea. You should also track every piece of extra income that you receive, and feel grateful for how it is adding to your deposit fund. Make a tracker of every £100 you save towards your goal and how much you have left to save. Being really on top of your goal and knowing where you are at will help you to stay focused. If you are having trouble thinking about what your ideal home is or you have blockages around what you think you deserve and what you can achieve, then the journal prompts for this month will help you out. Do these before you set your goals and view a house to really ensure you are going for what you want rather than what society paints as 'the ideal home'.

Journal prompts for figuring out your home goals

1. In what space in your current home do you feel most relaxed?

2. If you don't have anywhere that you currently feel most relaxed, how do you imagine your dream space where you *could* relax?

3. What colours make you feel relaxed?

4. If money was unlimited, what is one luxury item you would like in your home and why? Is it because it would make life easier? Is it because it will make you feel rich?

5. Out of all the places you have lived, where has felt the most like home to you, and why is that? Write about it.

6. What are your limiting beliefs that are stopping you from having your ideal home?

7. Do you think someone like you could ever live in your ideal home? Write about it.

8. If you could decorate your dream home, what colour interior would you go for?

9. Do you visualise living in your dream home alone? If yes, why, and if not, who do you envision living there with?

10. Would you like to have a garden? If so, how would you spend your time there? Would you do any gardening? Would you have people over for barbeques?

11. What are your favourite memories from your childhood home and what are your favourites from your current one, and how do they relate?

12. What sort of neighbourhood would you like to live in? How do you get on now with your current neighbours?

13. What is important to you to have on your doorstep?

14. Would you like to live somewhere amid the hustle and bustle?

15. Would you like to live in the countryside and why?

16. Is it important to live somewhere close to family and friends?

17. Are the schools around your ideal home important to you?

18. Would you like to host parties in your ideal home?

19. Would you have people round for Sunday roasts?

20. Would you spend a lot of time in your kitchen? If so, is the kitchen size important to you?

21. What is the best home you have ever visited? What did you like about it?

22. Did your childhood house feel cosy to you? How did this make you feel?

23. What marks would you make on your ideal home so that it felt like home?

24. Would you have wooden floors or carpets?

25. Would you like a room that you can dedicate just to you having your own time out?

Manifesting your dream home using visualisation

Now, remember those homes that you saved on Rightmove? I want you to print these off and place them on your vision board, so that you are being reminded of these houses daily and getting excited each time you see them. Of course, houses don't stay on the market for ever, so make sure that you find some similar houses on Google to what you want and post them on there too. *The Secret* shares the story of an entrepreneur who, when he first found out about the concept of a vision board, he decided to create some and he put huge goals such as the watch he wanted, the house he wanted, his dream car; it was totally unrealistic! He moved house three times after that and had put the vision boards into storage. Then three years later he moved into a house and his son was kicking at the boxes. His son asked, 'Daddy, what is in the boxes?' and he said 'vision boards', to which the child replied, 'What's a vision board?' So the dad opened the boxes to show him and then he started to cry, because, to his surprise, the dream house he put on his vision board years ago was the exact same house that he was living in. Not something similar, not the same house but in a different location, but the exact same house in the same location, and he'd done this all without even realising. So, dream big, and don't feel restricted to only putting the houses that you found on Rightmove on there. Remember that target figure you set yourself of extra income each month? You are going to write that in big on your vision board so that this goal is a prominent reminder every day that you are aiming to make that extra a month and your subconscious mind will be looking out for ways for you to receive this.

Now, you may be settled in your current home and not thinking about moving anytime soon, or ever, but that doesn't mean that you can't use your vision board to manifest your dream home. A home is more than its exterior, it's about how you make the house a home. Are you feeling like you are getting a bit tight for space? Would you like to convert your spare room into an office or a dressing room? Is your interior reminding you of some bad times that you experienced in that home? Would you like to create a nice place in your garden to chill and be at peace with nature? Go back on to Pinterest and search through the pins that you have pinned on your 'I am so grateful for my dream home' board, print these off and put them on your vision board. You can also add the colour scheme you would like to go for, pieces of furniture that you would like, and so on. Be as creative as you can! And as always, every time you see this vision board, feel how excited it makes you, and trust that you have asked, you believe and you are going to receive!

The cinema method is perfect for manifesting your dream home, especially if you have been looking at visual images online, and you can be as wild as your imagination lets you. You should do the cinema method for twenty minutes before you go to bed or for twenty minutes when you wake up, when the subconscious part of your brain is most active. You can write everything down first if it helps you think of every single detail. So, I want you to imagine walking in your front door. What colour is the door? Is it at the front of the house? Is it at the side of the house? Once you walk through the front door, what do you see? Are there stairs? Are they in front of you? Are they to the left of you? Now walk into the corridor. Is it narrow, is it wide? How is it decorated? What colour schemes have you got going on? Where is the kitchen? What is the layout? Is it open plan? Do you have big windows? Small windows? A garden? How big is the garden?

What can you see out of the window? Now walk up the stairs, if you have them in your dream house. How many bedrooms are there? What size are they? Who lives in them? How many bathrooms does it have? Is there room for a bathtub? Think of your bedroom. What sort of bed do you have? What is the bedding on it like? Do you have enough room for a vanity table? Have you got pictures of your loved ones all around it? What does it feel like to wake up there every morning and look out the window? What side of the house is your bedroom on? And what can you see outside? How do you feel when you are in that house? Do you feel rich and full of abundance? How are your clothes reflecting this? Have you treated yourself to some nice matching pyjamas and thrown out that ex-boyfriend's T-shirt you used to wear purely because you didn't care if you got fake tan on it and it was comfy! Imagine you at your optimum. This will all come your way, just trust in the Universe.

Another way that you can use visualisation and objects is by buying small items for your dream home and getting prepared for the day you get where you want to be. This doesn't mean break the bank and go and by a new sofa, but buy small, cute things you see when you're walking round B&M or Ikea, such as a plant pot or a wax melt burner. By doing this you are taking the action towards your goal and the Universe will think that it is already happening and bring this manifestation to you quicker.

Manifesting your dream home using positive affirmations

I have selected some positive affirmations for you guys to use this month to help shift that negative mindset of never being able to achieve your dream home and reprogramme the subconscious part of your brain. I would recommend choosing a few specific affirmations to focus on saying repeatedly daily.

1. Thank you, Universe, for blessing me with my ideal home.

2. My ideal home is on its way to me.

3. I have found my ideal home.

4. I have the funds to live in my ideal home.

5. I am currently waking up in my cosy, warm bed and looking at my ideal bedroom around me.

6. I am sitting in the garden of my ideal home, and I can see [*say what you can see*].

7. I am so content in my ideal home.

8. My offer just got accepted for my ideal home!

9. I am so proud of myself for all that I have achieved.

10. My address is [*say address of ideal home, if you know it*].

11. I live in a neighbourhood where there is a sense of community and everyone looks out for each other.

12. I am surrounded by beautiful objects that have been bought with love in my home.

13. I am opening the door of my ideal home.

14. My new home is magical and magnificent.

15. I live in the countryside and love going for country walks.

16. I am safe, relaxed and at peace in my ideal home.

17. There is nothing I love more than coming home after a long day.

18. I am busy creating happy memories with my family in our home.

19. My home is full of love.

20. It is easy for me to attract my dream home.

21. I absolutely love my new flat!

22. The time is right, the buyer is right, my house is SOLD.

23. I welcome creative guidance from the Universe.

24. I trust that I am being guided towards my dream home.

25. I think positively and bring a new house into existence.

Manifesting your dream home using scripting

Of course, this month our 3-6-9 scripting method is going to be dedicated to manifesting our ideal home, and there are two ways of doing this method. The first way that you can use 3-6-9 method is by thinking of the thing that you want, so this could be the name of your dream home, the name of the extension that you want, or the area you want to live in, and writing this down 3 times. Then think of the action related to your ideal home, so having an offer accepted, for example, and write this down 6 times. Lastly think of the emotion that you will feel once your manifestation comes to fruition and write this down 9 times. Do this in one sitting and every day, if possible. You can make this relevant to your own dreams and desires but here is an example of one you can use to manifest buying your dream home:

[insert the number of bedrooms] bedroom house in [insert area]

[insert the number of bedrooms] bedroom house in [insert area]

[insert the number of bedrooms] bedroom house in [insert area]

My offer was accepted on the [insert the number of bedrooms] bedroom house in [insert area].

My offer was accepted on the [insert the number of bedrooms] bedroom house in [insert area].

My offer was accepted on the [insert the number of bedrooms] bedroom house in [insert area].

My offer was accepted on the [insert the number of bedrooms] bedroom house in [insert area].

My offer was accepted on the [insert the number of bedrooms] bedroom house in [insert area].

My offer was accepted on the (insert the number of bedrooms) bedroom house in (insert area).

My offer was accepted on the [insert the number of bedrooms] bedroom house in [insert area] and I am jumping with joy.

My offer was accepted on the [insert the number of bedrooms] bedroom house in [insert area] and I am jumping with joy.

My offer was accepted on the [insert the number of bedrooms] bedroom house in [insert area] and I am jumping with joy.

My offer was accepted on the [insert the number of bedrooms] bedroom house in [insert area] and I am jumping with joy.

My offer was accepted on the [insert the number of bedrooms] bedroom house in [insert area] and I am jumping with joy.

My offer was accepted on the [insert the number of bedrooms] bedroom house in [insert area] and I am jumping with joy.

My offer was accepted on the [insert the number of bedrooms] bedroom house in [insert area] and I am jumping with joy.

My offer was accepted on the [insert the number of bedrooms] bedroom house in [insert area] and I am jumping with joy.

My offer was accepted on the [insert the number of bedrooms] bedroom house in [insert area] and I am jumping with joy.

The second way of using the 3-6-9 method is to write down an affirmation of the thing you want with the action and the emotion – for example, 'My offer was accepted on the [insert the number of bedrooms] bedroom house in [insert area] and I am jumping with joy' – then write this down 3 times in the morning, 6 times at lunchtime and 9 times in the evening.

Or you could choose one of the positive affirmations listed earlier. Each time you write it down you need to be present and really feel how you would feel when your manifestation does come true.

Once you have completed the 3-6-9 method, remember to breathe in and out; you have asked, you believe and now you will receive.

Another method that you can use to manifest your dream home is going back to the house or the apartment block that you book-marked and write on envelopes your name and the address of the home that you are manifesting. You should do this as often as possible, and soon enough your subconscious will believe that this is your address and your brain will be working in every way that it can to make that your home. Make sure that when you open the letters that you feel excited, and that you feel like it is your reality now to live there.

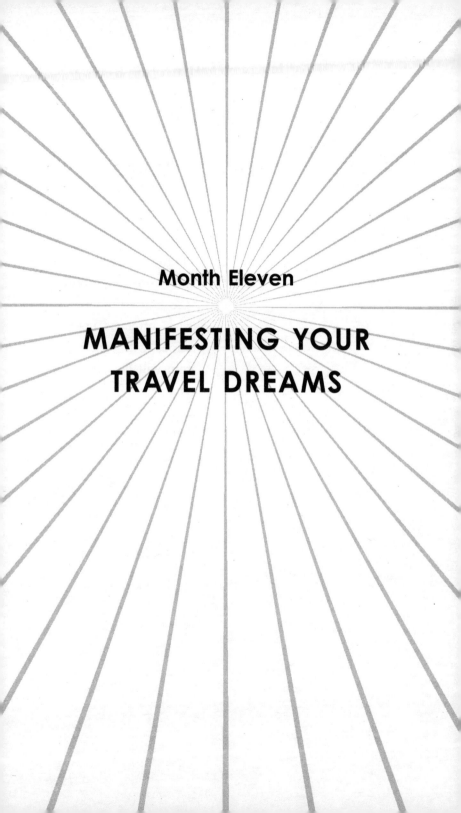

Month Eleven

MANIFESTING YOUR TRAVEL DREAMS

Welcome to month eleven, my queens, and nearly a whole year of manifesting, if you have been following this guide in chronological order. How does it feel? How has your life changed? How has the law of attraction bettered your life? Make sure you let me know by sending me a direct message over on Instagram @alanis_cooper. So, this month's topic is all about travel, something that since March 2020 has been very difficult for all of us to do. A holiday is needed every now and then (I wish I could go on holiday for six months twice a year!), as it is a great escape from reality and can help us to destress. Holidays are also where a lot of good memories are made with the people we love. How many of you have funny stories that you still tell from your travels from years ago, or fond memories of your childhood family holidays? Travel may be an area that you are lacking in your life right now and this month we are going to change that. I have to admit, I do go on a few holidays a year, but I haven't been travelling properly just yet, and it is definitely something that I will be focusing on manifesting once I am a qualified chartered accountant (yes, I'm qualifying as a chartered accountant!). I have heard such amazing stories from friends and families who have said it was the best thing they have ever done in their life.

There are so many reasons why I want to travel and I am sure these may appeal to you too. One of the main reasons is to escape daily London life, constantly being on the go, constantly in traffic, seeing the same people every time I go out. Travelling will break the cycle and broaden my mindset through my exploring new places, meeting new people, and making the most out of the budget I give myself. It will make me appreciate the people I have left behind and allow me to take a step back and look at my life. Another benefit to travelling is it can help to improve your communication skills, because you encounter new cultures and new languages. Also, you have so many new experiences, which gives you much to talk about when meeting up with family and friends and when you meet new people. You really get to discover yourself on a deeper level when you travel. First of all your ability to adapt to change really strengthens; you're often out of your comfort zone and then, once you get comfortable in one place and just start to find your bearings and meet your people, you're off again and need to adapt to a new place, or a new country and the way that they do life there. You also get to learn a lot about what you like and what you don't like, and that comes down to people, the food, the weather, activities, and many more things – it is all part of a process of finding yourself. You will carry the memories that you make while travelling for ever, even if you experience these on your own or with people who live halfway round the world from you. These memories will last a lifetime and form part of your identity, and you will tell your tales to your grandkids years from now. Your travelling goals may be completely different to mine. You may have never been on a plane before and wish to fly to the other side of the UK and go on holiday there, you may wish to go to the Maldives and stay in a luxury villa on the sea, you may just wish to be able to go on a staycation in the UK with the whole of your family.

There may be various blocks standing in between you and your travel goals, such as finances, time off work, fear of going alone if you are struggling to find company, or just not having the time to figure it out. So, as always, before we set our goals for the new area of travel, we are going to do some self-reflection work and journaling. I have listed some journal prompts that you should work through this month to find out what your goals are, to really figure out how you feel about travel and to get rid of those limiting beliefs and blockages that stand in the way of your travel dreams and desires!

Journal prompts for figuring our your travel goals

1. Describe a memory from the first trip you can remember?

2. Did you go away a lot as a child? Do you have fond memories?

3. Would you say you are well travelled? And why?

4. Describe your ideal vacation.

5. What are your thoughts on flying?

6. Has travelling ever appealed to you? If so, why haven't you ever been?

7. How do you feel about travelling solo?

8. Where is the best country you have ever visited and why? Detail the trip.

9. What is one country you would love to visit but have never got the chance to?

10. Do you think you will go travelling one day?

11. Would you miss home if you went travelling?

12. Do you ever feel like you are stuck in the same old town, with the same people, doing the same thing?

13. Can you speak another language? Would you like to?

14. Do you prefer city breaks or a beach holiday?

15. When you go on holiday, what are you going for?

16. What limiting beliefs do you have over allowing yourself to spend a lot of money on travel?

17. How does the quote 'money will return, but the memories won't' make you feel?

18. If you were stuck on a desert island, what three items would you take?

19. Do you prefer a party holiday or a relaxing holiday?

20. Have you ever been camping? Detail your experience.

21. How do you feel about living in another country?

22. What culture would you like to experience?

23. Would you like to work abroad?

24. Do you prefer a staycation or going abroad?

25. What is one country you've visited that you wouldn't return to?

After doing some self-reflection work, you should have identified what your goals are and what was holding you back. Now you need to take some action. If you had some limiting beliefs around finance, face your fears and actually look at the price that the holiday, staycation, or period travelling would cost you. Shop around, look at connecting flights to see if you can get money off, look at deals and come up with a rough figure. Then you need to write this figure down, saying: 'I am going to have

X amount spare income that I am going to use to fulfil my travel dreams and desires.' Just put it out there, stop delaying it! Then look at your budget for each month and how much spare income you have and work out what you can put away for this, and every time that you do put money away, say thank you to the Universe for giving you this money to fulfil your travel plans. And every time that you get any extra income, put this away as well and note mentally that the Universe brought this to you to fulfil your travel desires. If your limiting belief was not having the time, then make yourself look at your work commitments and see how you can offload some of these for a period of time, or speak to your manager and see if prolonged leave is something that they offer. You could even consider taking a career break! If the fear of going away on your own is stopping you, then maybe book a night away on your own and see how you find it; hopefully you will realise that you can do it and that there isn't anything to be scared about.

Manifesting your travel dreams using visualisation

Once you have set your goals for the type of travel you would like to manifest into your life, it is time to start manifesting. Print off pictures of the hotel, the countries, the area that you would like to travel to, and place these on your vision board, feeling the excitement of knowing that you will be there soon. Write on your vision board the figure that you need to be able find to fund your trip and place it next to the pictures, so this becomes prominent in your mind that this is the income you need for your travels. Print off pictures of activities you would like to do on your travels; whether it's camping, swimming with sharks, feeding elephants, jet skiing, or sunbathing and sipping cocktails, make them specific to you and your desires. If it is a flight that you would like to manifest, you could even print off a fake boarding pass (you can find templates online by searching 'blank boarding pass') and fill it out with your name, the date and the destinations that you would like to fly to, and stick that on your vision board!

Now we can of course use my favourite visualisation method, the cinema method – imagine how creative you can get when it comes to visualising your travel goals! You should do the cinema method for twenty minutes before you go to bed or for twenty minutes when you wake up, when the subconscious part of your brain is most active. This is something I actually used to do long before I knew I was manifesting. If ever I couldn't sleep, I used to close my eyes and think good thoughts about being on my dream holiday, usually with someone I had crush on, to help me sleep – and now that crush is my boyfriend of two years and we are flying to the place I always used to think about two days after I am writing this! So, close your eyes, and imagine watching yourself on screen on your dream holiday, travelling or whatever it may be. How excited you are! How proud of yourself you are for getting the money together to go and for removing all those limiting beliefs! Can you hear the sound of your suitcase dragging along the floor in the airport, or are you wearing a backpack full of travelling gear, or are you loading a van with your camping equipment? Who are you with? Are you alone? Are you with family? Are you with the love of your life? Allow yourself to get excited for the day this becomes your reality.

Manifesting your travel dreams using positive affirmations

Here are some positive affirmations for you to repeat daily throughout the month to speak your travel goals into reality and to shift your mindset to them being attainable:

1. The Universe is bringing my travel desires to me.

2. I am open and ready to travel.

3. I welcome new experiences.

4. I am determined to live my life to the fullest.

5. I am on my dream trip surrounded by my family and people I love.

6. Travel is a luxury that I deem important in my best life.

7. I am receiving so many opportunities to travel.

8. I enjoy the process of planning my dream trip.

9. I have great company to travel with.

10. I have experienced many new cultures and ways of life.

11. Travelling has opened my eyes to the bigger world out there.

12. Travel allows me to find myself.

13. Travel is an investment.

14. I am not my anxiety, I will be safe.

15. The world is my oyster.

16. I can explore anywhere I want and the resources for travel are always available to me.

17. I am grateful for any opportunity to travel.

18. I have unlimited choices.

19. I am grateful for safe journeys.

20. I love exploring new places.

21. I am open to meeting people who live a different lifestyle to me.

22. I am sitting on the balcony, overlooking the sea and waiting to get ready to go out for dinner.

23. As I allow more abundance and love into my life, more doors will open.

24. I am adaptable to different environments.

25. I am open to meeting new people.

Manifesting your travel dreams using scripting

Now for the 3-6-9 method, which you want to do every day, if possible. First write the type of travel you want to experience 3 times, then what you do there 6 times and lastly write how this makes you feel 9 times. Here is an example of how you can do this:

[Insert the destination]

[Insert the destination]

[Insert the destination]

I have travelled to [insert the destination], and I am having a relaxing holiday.

I have travelled to [insert the destination], and I am having a relaxing holiday.

I have travelled to [insert the destination], and I am having a relaxing holiday.

I have travelled to [insert the destination], and I am having a relaxing holiday.

*I have travelled to [insert the destination], and
I am having a relaxing holiday.*

*I have travelled to [insert the destination], and
I am having a relaxing holiday.*

*I have travelled to [insert the destination], and
I am having a relaxing holiday. This makes me feel
blessed and grateful for my life.*

*I have travelled to [insert the destination], and
I am having a relaxing holiday. This makes me feel
blessed and grateful for my life.*

*I have travelled to [insert the destination], and
I am having a relaxing holiday. This makes me feel
blessed and grateful for my life.*

*I have travelled to [insert the destination], and
I am having a relaxing holiday. This makes me feel
blessed and grateful for my life.*

*I have travelled to [insert the destination], and
I am having a relaxing holiday. This makes me feel
blessed and grateful for my life.*

*I have travelled to [insert the destination], and
I am having a relaxing holiday. This makes me feel
blessed and grateful for my life.*

*I have travelled to [insert the destination], and
I am having a relaxing holiday. This makes me feel
blessed and grateful for my life.*

*I have travelled to [insert the destination], and
I am having a relaxing holiday. This makes me feel
blessed and grateful for my life.*

*I have travelled to [insert the destination], and
I am having a relaxing holiday. This makes me feel
blessed and grateful for my life.*

The other way that you can use the 3-6-9 method is to write down an affirmation of the thing you want with the action and the emotion – for example, 'I have travelled to [insert the destination], and I am having a relaxing holiday. This makes me feel blessed and grateful for my life' – then write this down 3 times in the morning, 6 times at lunchtime and 9 times in the evening. You could also use one of the positive affirmations from the list earlier. This may be a better method for you if you struggle to stay present when doing the first method, as it is done in short intervals, which can allow you to maintain focus and to really feel the excitement of your manifestation coming to fruition.

Another scripting method that you can use is to write yourself a diary encounter reflecting on your trip. You should include everything that you got up to, how you found the experience, what your takeaways are and how you are feeling now that it is over.

Month Twelve

MANIFESTING YOUR SPECIFIC GOALS

This month we are going to focus on manifesting your own specific goals, which could be absolutely anything, from a specific exam result, winning a competition, passing your driving test, getting an offer accepted on your home, or whatever it is that your heart desires! I want you to think of one thing that you wish for that seems impossible to reach. Even if you have no idea how you are going to get there, by focusing on having it in your life this month, the Universe will do the rest and opportunities will start to arise and it will soon become very clear how you are going to get this manifestation into your life.

If you can't think of one specific thing that you would like to manifest this month, do not stress; this is what our journaling is for, to discover what it is that you really want. When thinking of your specific thing, ask yourself why. Why do you want to manifest this? How will this make you feel? Ensure that you are thinking about how having this thing in your life will make you feel, and how it will benefit you. Try to choose something that will have a long-term benefit rather than just a quick fix; for example, manifesting passing your driving test may give you a short-term feeling of pride and relief, but it will also provide long-term benefits like having more independence to go where you want, when you want, being able to save money on taxis and it can also open up opportunities in different areas of the country that you may not have been able to travel to before. Also think about how you are going to act once you have manifested your desire. For example, if it is a new pair of shoes that you have really wanted, will it make you feel more powerful and therefore likely to go for opportunities that you have never gone for before; if you wanted to manifest working with a specific brand for a huge amount of money, how will you act once you have the money? Will you be generous and give to charity? Will you give yourself a wardrobe upgrade and eat healthier? Try to keep all of this in mind when choosing what specific thing it is that you want to bring into your life.

You may be in the position where you have absolutely no clue what it is that you want to manifest into your life, so the journal prompts for this month should be able to help you with figuring out what it is that you want.

Journal prompts for figuring out your specific goals

1. The reason why you want this specific thing is _____

2. Once you have this specific thing, you will feel _____

3. This specific thing will change your life by _____

4. The thing standing in between you and this specific thing is _____

5. You can take a step closer today to this specific thing by _____

6. How long have you wanted this for? Why has it taken you this amount of time?

7. If you could swap one thing in your life for this, it would be _____

8. Are there any negatives to you getting this specific thing, and if so, why do you still want this?

9. When you look at your wheel of life, what area do you need to spend more time on?

10. Is there anything specific that you can think of in that area of your life that you could manifest to improve it?

11. What is one thing you have always wanted but always thought was out of reach?

12. What is one thing that would bring you long-term happiness?

13. What limiting beliefs do you have around the one thing that would make you happy?

14. Write down why you are worthy of having the one thing in your life that would make you happy.

15. Write down three things that you love about yourself.

16. Write down three ways that you could get the thing that you want.

17. If you had one wish in life, what would you wish for?

18. Write a list of people that you are envious of because of the stuff that they have in their life. Detail why for each one. And then detail what you could do to have the things that they have.

19. Finish this sentence: my life would be complete if I had _____

20. Have you ever tried to manifest this specific goal before? Did you lack the 'belief' that it would come to you? What will you do different this month when manifesting it?

21. Who would you tell first when this specific thing comes to fruition?

22. How will you receive this thing that you want? Document this happening.

23. Describe your family and friends' reaction to you receiving what you want.

24. Think about a specific thing in your life that you wanted in the past and that you received. How did this make you feel? How did you act?

25. Think about a specific thing in your life that you wanted in the past that you didn't receive. How did this make you feel? How did you act?

Manifesting your specific goals using visualisation

The whole point of visualisation is having a prominent visual reminder of your goals so that you are not losing sight of what they are, and you are reminding the Universe constantly about what it is you want so it can highlight ways for you to bring this into your life. A way that you can do this is by setting your password on your phone as the specific thing that you want. For example, if it is to pass an exam, you could change your phone password to: 'I have passed', writing this in the present tense as if it has already happened so that the Universe can mirror and reflect this into your life. Then every time you log into your phone you are manifesting without even realising! Another thing that you can do is set daily reminders on your laptop or phone, which could be something like: 'I am so proud of you for passing your exam.' Again you are getting that constant reminder that you are going to pass and putting it out into the Universe. Another thing that you can do is print off pictures of the specific thing you want to manifest and place them on your vision board. For example, if you want to manifest a specific grade in an exam, then what you can do is screen-grab a picture of the way that you receive your exam results, such as on a website, and using an editing app such as Canva, edit your desired result on to there, print this off, and place it on your vision board. Now remember, queens, when doing our vision boards it is important that we feel absolutely everything that we would feel if we were to receive this result, so that we can give off a high frequency that the Universe can tune in to.

We can also use the cinema method to manifest our specific goals, and we should do this for twenty minutes before we go to bed or for twenty minutes after we wake up, when our subconscious mind is the most active. Close your eyes and imagine you are at the cinema; the film is about to begin, you turn your phone off, sit back, get ready for the film to start rolling. The film on the screen is your manifestation coming to fruition, so, for example, if you were trying to manifest an offer on a house being accepted, you would visualise the moment when you find out. Where will you be? Who would you be with? What are you wearing? Now think about the person who is delivering this news. What is their name? How do they deliver the news? Do they do this by phone? Email? What do they sound like? What words do they use? Now think about what you do once you receive the news that your specific manifestation is happening. Who do you tell? How do you act? Do you post it on social media? If so, what do you say? Be as descriptive as you possibly can and really feel the emotions that you would feel when it comes true. Now, as always once we have finished our manifestation, we need to take a deep breath, let go and trust in the Universe's divine timing.

Manifesting your specific goals using positive affirmations

Choose a couple of these positive affirmations to repeat daily each week. You can incorporate these into your daily routine when you are taking a shower, or on your way to work, and you can even record them and play them on a loop to listen to on your commute or while working.

1. I don't chase, I attract. What is meant for me will find me.

2. I am worthy of good things.

3. What is meant for me won't pass me by.

4. My life is filled with happiness and joy.

5. I am on track to getting what I want.

6. I will have everything I have ever wanted this year.

7. Good things are coming.

8. I have [say your specific thing] in my life.

9. I am grateful for [say specific thing] in my life.

10. I am working with the Universe to bring [say specific thing] into my life.

11. I am a magnet for my dreams and goals.

12. I am present.

13. I am wealthy in every area of my life.

14. I am creating my own destiny.

15. Thank you, Universe, for always bringing me what I want.

16. Thank you, Universe, for making me amazing enough to make my dreams a reality.

17. I am creative, and always find a way to get what I want.

18. The Universe has my back.

19. I am ready to live my dream life.

20. I am abundant.

21. My subconscious mind is always working on ways I can achieve what I want.

22. I am grateful for all the lessons that I have learnt in my life that have made me the person that I am today.

23. I am surrounded by people who want me to do well.

24. I am surrounded by like-minded successful people.

25. All manifestations come to me easily.

Manifesting your specific goals using scripting

Using the 3-3-3 or 5-5-5 method

You can use the 3-3-3 or the 5-5-5 method to manifest your specific goal by choosing a positive affirmation from the previous page and writing this down either 33 times for 3 days or 55 times for 5 days. The key to this is ensuring that you are present in the moment while writing this down and giving out the energetic frequency that you will feel when your manifestations become reality.

Using the 3-6-9 method

You could also use the 3-6-9 scripting method and there are two ways that you can do this. The first is to write the specific thing that you want 3 times, the action to do with it 6 times, and the emotion that you will feel once you have it 9 times. An example of this is below:

Driver's licence

Driver's licence

Driver's licence

I have passed my driving test and got my driver's licence.

I have passed my driving test and got my driver's licence.

I have passed my driving test and got my driver's licence.

I have passed my driving test and got my driver's licence.

I have passed my driving test and got my driver's licence.

I have passed my driving test and got my driver's licence.

I have passed my driving test and got my driver's licence and I feel proud of myself.

I have passed my driving test and got my driver's licence and I feel proud of myself.

I have passed my driving test and got my driver's licence and I feel proud of myself.

I have passed my driving test and got my driver's licence and I feel proud of myself.

I have passed my driving test and got my driver's licence and I feel proud of myself.

I have passed my driving test and got my driver's licence and I feel proud of myself.

I have passed my driving test and got my driver's licence and I feel proud of myself.

I have passed my driving test and got my driver's licence and I feel proud of myself.

I have passed my driving test and got my driver's licence and I feel proud of myself.

You can use this template and make it relevant to whatever your specific goal is. Repeat this every day, if possible, or at least a couple of times a week. Be sure that once you have finished this practice that you breathe in and out, let go and trust the Universe.

The second way is to write down one positive affirmation that's to do with your specific goal, 3 times in the morning, 6 times at lunchtime and then 9 times in the evening. Each time you come back to do your practice, make sure you are present in the moment.

Moving forward

So, my queens, what a journey we have been on together. From learning the basics of manifesting to where you are at now, I bet your life has changed incredibly and I am so proud of you. There may have been a few setbacks along the way, and times where you were totally ready to give up your manifesting journey altogether, but the Universe supported you and put you back on the path that you are meant to be on, and I bet that you are so glad that it did. I want you to reflect back on the position that you were in when you started this book and where you are now. Do you still want the stuff that you manifested back then? Have your plans for your dream life changed? How much of what you wanted to manifest came to fruition? You have come such a long way in a year and your manifesting journey is just getting started! By now you should all be professional manifesting queens, and know all the ways that manifesting works best for you, whether it is visualisation, scripting, using crystals, using subliminals, using music or, like me, using a mixture of them all. That is the beauty of manifesting: there is no strict rule book to follow, as it is all about what feels right to you, what raises your vibration the best, and also what you have the time and energy for. But you owe it to yourself to make manifesting a top priority in your life.

Now, just because this book is over, it doesn't mean that your journey with the law of attraction is too. Please use my tips for the rest of your life, and go on to teach the law of attraction to as many people as you can! Also, please keep in touch; my Instagram is @alanis_cooper and my TikTok is @alaniscooperx. I document my own law of attraction journey on there and can't wait to see yours. Thanks for reading. Peace out, my manifesting queens x.

Resources

A blank cheque that you can use to visualise money: *https://www.thesecret.tv/wp-content/uploads/2015/04/ the-magic-check-en.pdf*

Writing a letter to your future self: *www.dearfutureme.org*

Test to find your learning style: *https://vark-learn.com/the-vark-questionnaire*

Books

The Secret by Rhonda Byrne

The Magic by Rhonda Byrne

Get Rich, Lucky Bitch! by Denise Duffield-Thomas

*Rich as F*ck* by Amanda Frances

Podcasts

Goal Digging & Manifesting with Alanis
    – Alanis Cooper (my podcast!)

Law of Attraction Changed My Life – Francesca Amber

Miracle Mindsets – Sammie & Jen